GOLF
MAGAZINE

THE BEST
DRIVING
INSTRUCTION
BOOK EVER!

A SPORTS ILLUSTRATED PUBLICATION

© 2011 Time Home Entertainment Inc.

Published by Time Home Entertainment Inc.
135 West 50th Street
New York, N.Y. 10020

Some of the material in this book was previously
published in *Golf Magazine*, and
is reprinted with permission by Time Inc.

ISBN 10: 1-60320-211-0
ISBN 13: 978-1-60320-211-4
Library of Congress Control Number: 2011931184

Printed in China

We welcome your comments and suggestions about
Time Home Entertainment Inc. Books.
Please write to us at:
Time Home Entertainment Inc. Books
Attention: Book Editors
PO Box 11016
Des Moines, IA 50336-1016

If you would like to order any of our hardcover
Collector's Edition books,
please call us at (800) 327-6388
Monday through Friday: 7:00 a.m.- 8:00 p.m. CST;
Saturday: 7:00 a.m.- 6:00 p.m. CST

Cover/book design: Paul Ewen
Cover photography: Angus Murray

GOLF
MAGAZINE

THE BEST
DRIVING
INSTRUCTION
BOOK EVER!

Make the game easier with longer tee shots that never miss the fairway
using Tour-proven techniques from golf's top driving instructors

EDITED BY DAVID DENUNZIO

WITH THE
TOP 100 TEACHERS IN AMERICA

A SPORTS ILLUSTRATED PUBLICATION

YOUR GUIDE TO THE
ULTIMATE DRIVING EXPERIENCE

Hit it farther and straighter off the tee with a serious driving-improvement plan developed by the most elite collection of driving instructors and researchers the golf world has ever seen

Driving the ball less than 230 yards means that you'll score in the 90s often, somewhere in the 80s every once in a while, and never in the 70s. If you're fine with that, well, fine. Since you're holding this book in your hands, however, I have a sneaking suspicion that you're not, and that you consider your lack of pop off the tee a stumbling block along the path to the player you wish to be.

It used to be that players and instructors considered shots taken from 100 yards and in (and never those generated from the tee box) as the most important to scoring—an assessment borne from the fact that 60 percent of most amateurs' shots originate from short range. However, after realizing that many of these strokes were actually gimmees, and that most were the result of not driving the ball far enough to leave a manageable iron into the green, the golf community is looking at driving—and power—in a whole new light: The modern secret to scoring.

Plus, is there anything more fun about golf then stepping on the tee with the confidence of knowing that you can put it out there in the middle of the fairway, and deep enough to hit your approach with a scoring iron, or with enough distance to make hitting a par-5 green in two a realistic proposition? I, along with the instructors, researchers and fitness experts behind this book argue that anything else you do in your game doesn't come close.

GOLF Magazine packages dozens of lessons on driving in its pages every year—an issue-by-issue guide to hitting your tee shots longer, straighter and with more confidence. This book is different. It's the first of its kind, really, with a carefully calculated game plan to finding the motions and methods that will stop you from making the tee-ball mistakes you've been making, and instead pay heed to the time-proven techniques employed by the very best drivers on the professional tours. The strategy is thus:

1. Understand what's happening at impact and why your ball flies the way it does [*pages 8-17*].

2. Process this information to convince yourself that you need to develop a driver swing that's completely different than the one you use with your irons [*pages 20-29*].

3. Run through a carefully designed series of body movement and design tests to discover what type of swing best fits your build and ability.

There are thousands, but really only one that's perfectly fit for you [*pages 32-53*].

4. Hone your technique and further dial in your method, including the way you best control the clubface so that you get it to square when you make contact with the ball [*pages 56-101*].

5. Apply some fuel and consistency to your swing by targeting your strength, speed and mobility limitations, and improving them with moves that—maybe for the first time—tap the secret power sources within you [*pages 104-161*].

6. Groove your new technique with specially designed drills and routines that not only help you improve, but also make sure you take your best driver swings to the course [*pages 164-181*].

7. Maximize your yardage by learning how nailing your driver specs can help you create optimal launch conditions [*pages 182-189*].

An easy, 7-step plan (presented over the course of 10 chapters) developed by what's arguably the single greatest collection of driving experts ever assembled (check the bios on page 190-191). See you deep down the fairway.

DAVID DENUNZIO
INSTRUCTION EDITOR, GOLF MAGAZINE

CONTENTS

CHAPTER 1

Impact lasts less than 1/2,500th of a second, and it's the only thing that you do with your swing that the ball really cares about.

THE *SECRET* TO DRIVING SUCCESS

Getting in touch with how your clubface position and path at impact affect your drives is Step 1 in your quest to dominate off the tee

By **JAMES LEITZ, PGA**
Pinewood C.C., Slidell, La.

YOU HEAR IT ALL OF THE TIME: "Impact means everything." It does, especially when hitting driver. In fact, playing golf boils down to your ability to control the collision between your clubhead and the ball to produce a desired result. When your impact is correct, the game is easy. If you've ever played in a "Shamble" where everybody in your foursome tees off then selects the best drive to complete the hole, then you know what I mean. Playing from position "A" gives you a good shot at birdie on every hole.

It doesn't matter what model driver you swing or what your motion looks like, the ball responds only to the instructions it gets at impact, which have been difficult for instructors to nail down in the past because it happens so fast. The amount of time the ball spends in contact with the clubface is only 0.4 milliseconds. To put this number in perspective, imagine you shoot 90 during your next round. The total impact time for those 90 swings and strokes is 36 milliseconds. Hard to believe, but your entire round is determined in a little under 1/30th of a second.

In this book you're going to learn a lot about your physical capabilities, why your base structural strengths and limitations determine how you should swing, and the modifications you can make to your equipment to get the most yards from your motion. My job in this chapter is to tell you that all of this information won't mean a thing until you understand what's happening at impact. The fact that most golfers don't have a clue about the proverbial "Moment of Truth" explains why amateurs have difficulty finding the fairway and producing sufficient distance. The problem is exacerbated by the design of the club itself.

Why is the driver so hard to hit? *A few reasons:*

1. It moves faster through impact than any other club in your bag. This allows it to produce the most distance, but also requires your impact to be more precise.

2. It's the longest club you own, meaning that the impact point you so desperately need to control is farthest away from you.

3. At about 200 grams, your driver clubhead is the lightest you carry. Because of this, it tends to twist more on off-center hits

4. It's your lowest lofted full-swing club, and less loft means less forgiveness.

5. Its Center of Gravity sits back from the clubface, introducing Gear Effect when you make contact away from the sweet spot—shots hit toward the toe fly more to the left than if they were hit in the center (the opposite is true when you hit the ball off the heel). The majority of your accuracy problems are likely due to heel or toe impact.

As you're about to find out, learning how to produce the correct impact positions makes hitting your driver and producing solid tee shots much less difficult.

THE SCIENCE OF IMPACT

Impact alignments and resulting ball flight are controlled by physics and geometry. Physics and geometry never take a day off from the course. For some, that's bad news, but for others it's good news. In other words, the laws that punish bad shots are the same laws that reward you with good shots.

The primary impact alignments (or impact factors) that have the most affect on your drives are as follows.

Your clubface angle and clubhead path at impact determine the direction your drives travel, good or bad.

IMPACT FACTOR 1: Clubhead Path

The path of the clubhead best described as the direction of the motion of the club's Center of Gravity at impact. This direction of motion exists in both horizontal and vertical planes. The horizontal component describes how far to the left or right of the target line the club is moving, and the vertical component measures if the clubhead is ascending or descending as it attacks the ball.

IMPACT FACTOR 2: Clubface Angle

The clubface angle at impact (i.e., where your clubface is pointing) is the most important impact alignment when it comes to accuracy. It influences up to 75 percent of the direction the ball starts when it and the path aren't in sync, and up to 85 percent with a driver. For example, if your clubhead path is 10 degrees to the right of the target line, but your clubface is square to the target line (0 degrees), then the ball will start only 2 degrees to the right and then hook. Unfortunately, clubface angle is also the most difficult of the impact alignments to consistently repeat successfully.

IMPACT FACTORS 1 + 2 = A New Parameter Called D-Plane

n his book *The Physics of Golf* (1994), Dr. Theodore Jorgensen describes impact alignments as the "D-Plane" because they're *descriptive* of what happens during the collision between the clubhead and the ball. Variances in these impact alignments produce different ball speeds, launch angles, spin rates and, as a result, different shot patterns—some successful and some not.

A plane, as you're aware, forms when two lines intersect. In establishing the D-

Plane, one of these lines is the clubhead path. The other is the clubface angle, and as you can guess, the combination of the two can form an infinite number of D-Planes. When you make impact with the clubface aiming in the same direction that the clubhead is moving, the D-Plane is perfectly vertical, resulting in a straight shot. The D-Plane tilts when you get your clubface and path pointed in different directions, and a tilted D-Plane means the ball is going anywhere but straight on a center-face hit.

"A tilted D-Plane means the ball is going anywhere but straight on a center-face hit."

THE D-PLANE
The red line is the clubhead path (Impact Factor 1), which in this photo is moving both down the target line and slightly up. The yellow line represents clubface direction (Impact Factor 2). The plane formed between these two lines is the D-Plane.

CLUBFACE DIRECTION

D - PLANE

CLUBHEAD PATH

Learn more about D-Plane in a special video lesson with James Leitz at **golf.com/bestdrivingbook**

For instance, if your path is to the left of where your clubface is pointing at impact, your resultant D-plane will tilt to the right. The ball will start on this plane and, because it's spin axis sits perpendicular to the D-Plane, will curve to the right. A similar but opposite scenario occurs when your path is to the right of where your clubface is pointing at impact [*photos, below*].

If you've never read Dr. Jorgensen's book then this is probably the first time you've heard of D-Plane. That's because up until recently instructors didn't have the tools to accurately measure what's going on at impact. It was too fast for video and certainly too fast to be judged by the naked eye. Thanks to the TrackMan™ launch monitor (a Doppler-based radar that measures seven clubhead delivery parameters and 15 ball-flight measurements), instructors can now analyze impact as if it's happening in ultra-slow motion.

The D-Plane and You

So far I've talked about the D-Plane as a plane existing between the intersecting lines created by your clubface angle and clubhead path. Recall, however, that clubhead path includes both a horizontal and a vertical component, which you need to factor in to really understand how D-Plane affects you and your swing.

The only way to accurately describe what's happening is to map the sweet spot movement in at least three different places before and after impact. This forms your downswing swing plane, and where this plane intersects the ground is your plane direction. However, since the club-head path is determined by the movement of the sweet spot on this plane at the moment of impact in relation to the target line, then the only time clubhead path and the downswing plane point in the same direction is at the low point of your swing arc. For instance, say the base of your downswing plane is pointing down the target line as you attack the ball on a downward angle [*model, right*]. Notice how this creates a clubhead path that's moving to the right, or inside-out. If you're hitting up on the ball with the downswing plane pointing at the hole, then the clubhead path shifts to the left (outside in). The key is to adjust the downswing plane to the left or right of the target the correct amount to cancel out the clubhead path changes caused by hitting down or up on the ball.

HOW THE D-PLANE AFFECTS YOUR SHOTS

STRAIGHT

I'm using an iron model here but the effects of D-Plane apply to every club you own.

The spin axis of the ball (it can only rotate around one) is always perpendicular to the D-Plane. Thus, a vertical D-Plane produces a shot with zero axis tilt and a straight ball flight.

SLICE SPIN

When the path direction is left of where the clubface is pointing, the D-Plane is tilted to the right as is the spin axis. This causes the ball to curve to the right.

HOOK SPIN

When the path direction is right of where the clubface is pointing, the D-Plane is tilted to the left as is the spin axis. This causes the ball to curve to the left.

"The secret is to shift your downswing plane to the left or right when it's affected by the vertical component (angle of attack) of your club path."

What complicates this relationship is that the flatter the lie of the club the more dramatic adjustment. For example, at a 63-degree plane angle, which is a little flatter than the average 9-iron lie angle, a 2-degree downward angle of attack creates a 1-degree inside-out path. At a 45-degree plane angle, which is a little flatter than the lie angle of your driver, a 2-degree downward angle of attack creates a 2-degree inside-out path. Thus, with a driver, the path is most affected by hitting down or up.

The secret is to adjust your downswing plane to offset the vertical component of your path (angle of attack) by swinging outside-in when hitting down on the ball and swinging inside-out when hitting up on the ball. This will zero out your clubhead path get it moving toward the hole at impact. If you do this with your clubface aimed at the target while making contact in the center of the clubface, you'll produce a perfectly straight ball flight. You'll learn more about this with Dr. T.J. Tomasi in Chapter 2.

Watch the D-Plane models at right in action at
golf.com/bestdriving book

THE SECRET TO DRIVING THE BALL STRAIGHT

To help you better understand how to unlock the secrets of the D-Plane, I constructed a model that allows you to create different clubface angle and clubhead path patterns—and resulting D-Planes—at impact. The models' unique swivel design allows you to adjust the downswing plane to offset the fact that the clubhead path points to the right of the target when you hit down on the ball and to the left of the target when you hit up.

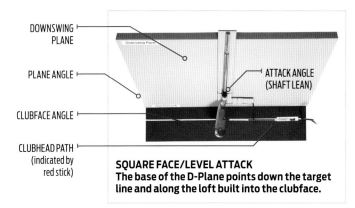

DOWNSWING PLANE

PLANE ANGLE

CLUBFACE ANGLE

CLUBHEAD PATH (indicated by red stick)

ATTACK ANGLE (SHAFT LEAN)

SQUARE FACE/LEVEL ATTACK
The base of the D-Plane points down the target line and along the loft built into the clubface.

ANGLE OF ATTACK

SWING PLANE ADJUSTMENT

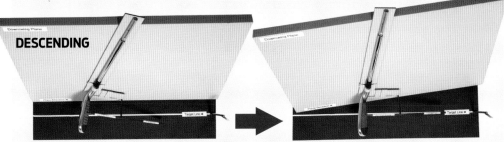

DESCENDING

When you approach impact on a descending arc (hitting down on the ball), the path of your clubhead is actually moving to the right.

ADJUSTMENT: SWING TO THE LEFT
Shifting your downswing plane to the left cancels out the inside-out movement.

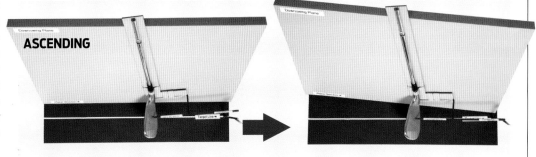

ASCENDING

When you approach impact on an ascending arc (hitting up on the ball), the path of your clubhead is actually moving to the left.

ADJUSTMENT: SWING TO THE RIGHT
Shifting your downswing plane to the right cancels out the outside-in movement.

IMPACT FACTOR 3: Clubhead Speed

The speed of your clubhead is the impact condition that has the greatest effect on distance. For every additional mile an hour of clubhead speed you can generate the ball will potentially travel three yards farther. In the past, clubhead speed was very difficult for a player to increase, but with the lessons you'll learn in this book and by building a swing that adheres to your body type the story is now much different.

One way to increase club speed is to use a longer and lighter shaft, but swinging a driver that's too light or long for you to control can sometimes *reduce* clubhead speed (which is why you need to seek out an experienced fitter and consult the guidelines presented in Chapter 10). Regardless of the adjustments you make to your equipment, your swing, or your body, measure your speed after each change to verify improvement or to see if in fact it's causing you to slow down.

Keep in mind that the faster you swing through impact, the more spin you'll produce. This can either be a good thing or a bad thing. Also, the faster your clubhead speed the more precise the other impact alignments must be for you to produce a straight ball flight.

IMPACT FACTOR 4: Impact Point

Where you contact the ball on the face heavily influences distance *and* direction because different contact points affect launch angle, ball speed and spin [*illustrations, opposite page*]. The directional effect of contact point is most severe with your driver because of the Gear Effect inherent in its design. Because the Center of Gravity in most modern drivers sits about an inch behind the face (and not in the face like it does on your irons), contact made away from the sweet spot causes the clubhead to twist radically. And since the clubhead can only rotate around its Center of Gravity, catching one on the toe will cause the clubhead to rotate clockwise, while making contact toward the heel will cause it to rotate counter-clockwise. The rotation is significant

"In the past, clubhead speed was very difficult for a player to increase, but with the lessons you'll learn in this book the story is now much different."

Clubhead speed and contact point heavily influence how far you hit your drives.

Learn how to make contact on the sweet spot every time at **golf.com/bestdrivingbook** enough to apply spin to the ball in the direction opposite of the head rotation. This is Gear Effect. It happens on any shot where you make contact away from the sweet spot, including points above and below the center as well as toward the heel and toe. Here's what you can expect:

TOE HIT: Draw or hook spin
HEEL HIT: Fade or slice spin
BELOW SWEET SPOT: Lower launch angle with higher spin
ABOVE SWEET SPOT: Higher launch angle with lower spin

HOW TO DIAL IN YOUR IMPACT POINT

Mark the face...

...and see where you made contact.

A dry erase marker is a great way to identify the location of your impact point. Purchasing one will be the best $1.50 you spend on your game.

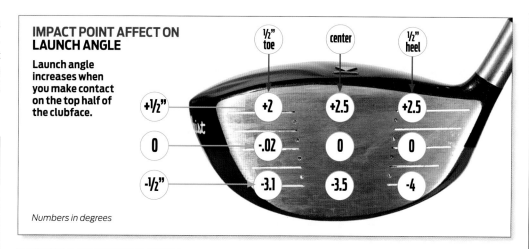

IMPACT POINT AFFECT ON LAUNCH ANGLE

Launch angle increases when you make contact on the top half of the clubface.

	½" toe	center	½" heel
+½"	+2	+2.5	+2.5
0	-.02	0	0
-½"	-3.1	-3.5	-4

Numbers in degrees

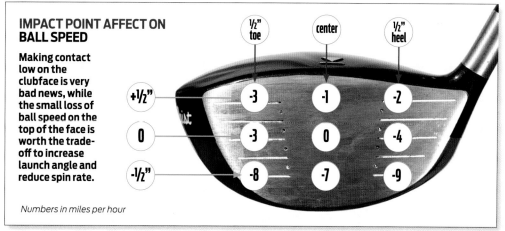

IMPACT POINT AFFECT ON BALL SPEED

Making contact low on the clubface is very bad news, while the small loss of ball speed on the top of the face is worth the trade-off to increase launch angle and reduce spin rate.

	½" toe	center	½" heel
+½"	-3	-1	-2
0	-3	0	-4
-½"	-8	-7	-9

Numbers in miles per hour

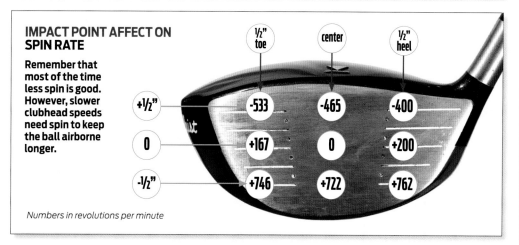

IMPACT POINT AFFECT ON SPIN RATE

Remember that most of the time less spin is good. However, slower clubhead speeds need spin to keep the ball airborne longer.

	½" toe	center	½" heel
+½"	-533	-465	-400
0	+167	0	+200
-½"	+746	+722	+762

Numbers in revolutions per minute

OPTIMIZING DRIVER PERFORMANCE

The first thing you should do before considering changing drivers or trying to maximize distance is to make sure you've eliminated the negative consequences of each Impact Factor. I've found that the best way to check progress is with face tape, or assessing the contact points left by the ball on a driver inked with a dry erase marker [*photos, opposite page*]. Eliminating these problems will solve many of your distance problems and all of your directional hang-ups. As far as your equipment is concerned, consult the Optimization Charts on page 189. This data provides you with key information as it relates to the launch angle and spin that are best for your swing. In order to use the Optimization Charts effectively, however, you must first determine your clubhead speed and angle of attack. The first one is easy—you can measure clubhead speed with many devices offered by your local pro shop. The second will take some effort as you'll need to get on a launch monitor to determine your angle of attack. You need to know your angle of attack because optimal launch angles and spin rates change depending on its value.

Also, it's important that you decide whether you want maximum carry or maximum distance (regardless of carry). You should base this decision on the conditions in which you typically play. If you play a really wet course then maximum carry is more important. If you play a firm or windy golf course then maximum distance (with extra roll) is more important. My opinion is that maximizing total distance is more efficient [*table, above*] unless you play in really soft conditions.

Lastly, consider the type of ball you use. If you normally create excess spin with your driver then playing anything but a lower-spinning ball will make hitting your optimal numbers difficult to achieve. Convincing a golfer, especially a low-handicap player, to use anything less than a premium, high-spin ball is difficult. Don't allow yourself to be so close-minded. Only play a high-spin ball if your measured swing data can back it up. ●

MAXIMIZING CARRY

Clubhead Speed	Angle of Attack	Launch Angle	Spin Rate	Carry Distance	Total Distance
100 MPH	5° UP	14.9°	2,538 RPM	247 yds.	284 yds.
100 MPH	0°	12.1°	3,118 RPM	235 yds.	272 yds.

MAXIMIZING TOTAL DISTANCE

Clubhead Speed	Angle of Attack	Launch Angle	Spin Rate	Carry Distance	Total Distance
100 MPH	5° UP	12.4°	1,887 RPM	239 yds.	293 yds.
100 MPH	0°	10.0°	2,570 RPM	230 yds.	278 yds.

Data courtesy TrackMan™

Optimal launch and spin change depending on whether you prioritize carry or overall distance.

A FINAL DISTANCE FACTOR: LANDING ANGLE

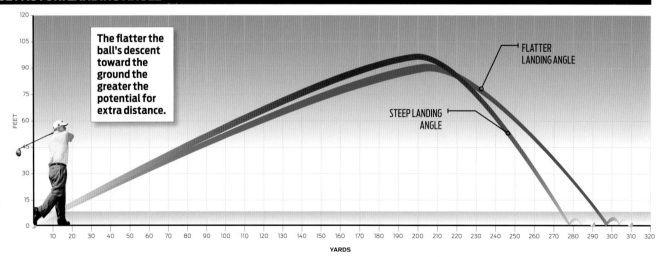

Instructors have known that a flatter landing angle was more advantageous than a steep one, but until TrackMan™ came along we didn't know the extent. For every degree you reduce the ball's descent you can add 1.5 to 2 yards. The trick: develop a draw. You can easily decrease your landing angle 10 degrees with a right-to-left ball flight.

The flatter the ball's descent toward the ground the greater the potential for extra distance.

FLATTER LANDING ANGLE

STEEP LANDING ANGLE

YARDS

"Make sure you've eliminated the negative consequences of each Impact Factor before considering changing drivers or trying to maximize distance."

5 THINGS TO TAKE FROM THIS CHAPTER

1 Optimize clubhead path, angle of attack, clubface direction, and impact point by improving your swing before changing club specifications.

2 Verify your clubhead delivery alignments at impact with a TrackMan™ launch monitor.

3 Driving the ball for distance is primarily a product of clubhead speed, but never compromise accuracy for small increases in yardage.

4 Decide whether you want to prioritize carry or overall distance based on your most common playing conditions.

5 Fit your driver to compliment the optimal launch angle and spin rate for your clubhead speed and angle of attack. This is an absolute must in order to take advantage of what modern technology can offer.

3-POST/MID-TRACK DRIVER
ERNIE ELS

Very few pure rotary (track-to-track) golfers hit it harder or sweeter

Ernie Els' tag as "The Big Easy" certainly fits. Yes, he's a big guy and, yes, his swing looks as smooth as silk. But make no mistake—Ernie hits the ball hard and he's been doing it consistently for the better part of 25 years.

The secret to generating his trademark power and accuracy is in your wrists. Notice how Els hinges them quickly and fully as he swings the club to the top [*Frame 4*]. When he lets the hinge out, it gives the appearance of swinging smoothly and without effort, even though his clubhead is blasting through impact at 120 mph.

At address, Ernie keeps his arms as soft as possible and kinks his right elbow slightly. This allows him to start the club back by hinging his wrists and bending his right elbow.

Note how quickly the shaft becomes parallel to the ground and perfectly set on his natural right-arm plane [*Frame 3*]. His free-and-easy wrist hinge and right-elbow fold places him on his shoulder plane at the top, but then he almost immediately drops back down to the mid-track position. He's a pure rotary (mid-track to mid-track) swinger [*see Chapter 3*].

Lastly, check Els' left hip—it's higher than his right at impact. He pulls it up and to the left using his powerful glutes. His arms and clubhead have no other option but to follow at breakneck speed and to send the ball deep down the fairway.

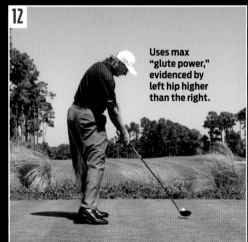

Uses max "glute power," evidenced by left hip higher than the right.

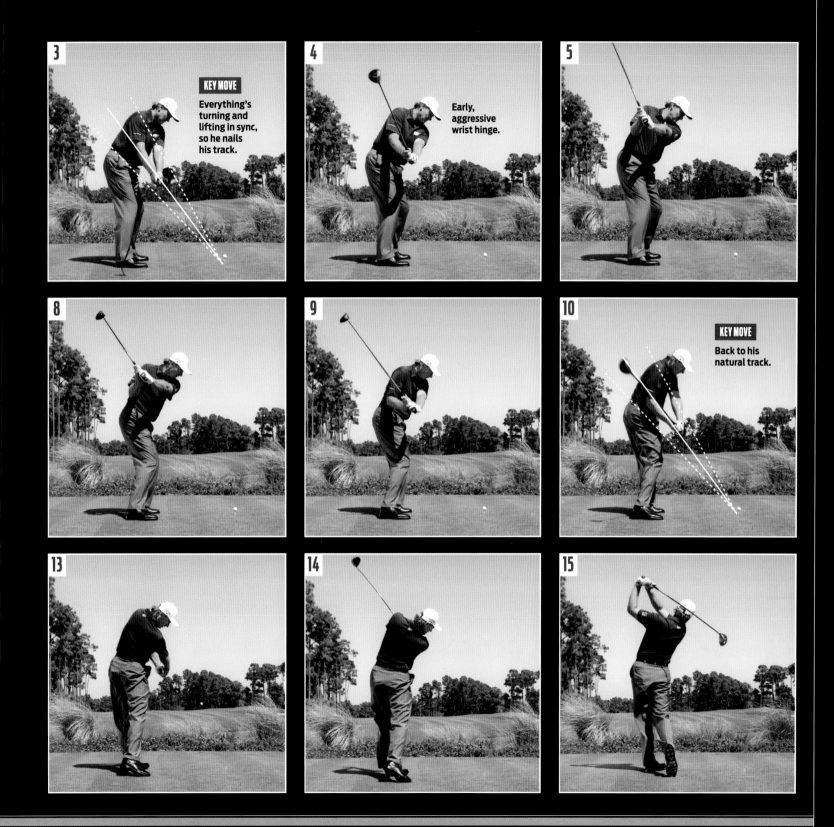

3

KEY MOVE

Everything's turning and lifting in sync, so he nails his track.

4

Early, aggressive wrist hinge.

5

8

9

10

KEY MOVE

Back to his natural track.

13

14

15

CHAPTER 2

How you deliver your driver into the ball is very—*very!*—different than the way you deliver your irons.

THE CASE FOR A *UNIQUE* DRIVER SWING

You tee the ball up when hitting your driver. This seemingly small difference from the swings you make when the ball is on the ground mandates an entirely different motion.

By **DR. T.J. TOMASI**, **PGA**
PGA Center for Golf Learning and Performance, Port St. Lucie, Fla.

SAM SNEAD ONCE TOLD A YOUNG Johnny Miller, "Son, you'll either be a great driver of the ball or a great iron player. Nobody is both."

Sage words that still ring true because if you take a look at your own game you'll notice that on some days you hit your irons like a seasoned Tour pro but drive the ball like you've never held a club before, and on others it's just the reverse. You'll also notice that the pattern is anything but random. It has a very defined structure. I call it the Continuum of Mediocrity, and like the name suggests, it's not a fun way of going about playing the game.

The problem with the Continuum is that sliding back and forth while you're trapped in it means that you're never maximizing your talent—one part of your game is always in decline while the other is on the rise. Throw in a balky short game and it's the rare golfer indeed who's consistently firing on all cylinders.

At the heart of the problem is a faulty base approach to playing golf: Most golfers think that they need only one swing for all of their clubs. As you'll learn, this dooms you to a lifetime of so-so, mostly unrewarding golf.

Why, over the hundreds of years that golf has been played, hasn't the Continuum been exposed? I propose three reasons:

1. It's common sense to use the same swing for all shots (but in this instance common sense is wrong).

2. The process of sliding back and forth on the Continuum is so slow that you can't recognize it—even when you're directly in the middle of it.

3. A proper measuring device to tell us that what we see with our naked eye isn't the entire story has only recently been developed. As one of America's best teachers, Martin Hall, points out: "What the eye can't see, the video sees. What the video can't see, TrackMan™ sees."

Like you've just read in Chapter 1, pinpointing what's happening at impact is absolutely key for improving performance, and that the manner in which you swing your clubhead into the ball (either with a descending, flat or ascending blow) has as much effect on the quality of your shots as your fundamentals at address and everything else you do in your swing. In fact, angle of attack demands that you have more than one swing in your bag, and is the answer to solving the Continuum for good.

The Continuum of Mediocrity
A simple explanation of why the game is so often frustrating.

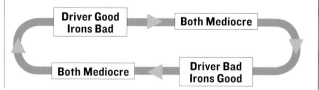

ONE SWING T | ANOTHER SWING

Your Swing: Under a Microscope

Modern extensions of the human eye such as TrackMan™ and other ball-flight measuring technologies show that clubface angle at impact accounts for approximately 85 percent of your shot's starting direction, while the clubhead path at impact contributes only 15 percent. They also have shown, as James Leitz touched on in the previous chapter, that the angle on which the clubhead approaches the ball (aka, angle of attack) is an impact variable far more important than previously supposed.

To hit the ball the farthest with your driver you need just the right balance between your ball speed, launch angle and spin rate. The key to maximizing distance is high launch and low spin coupled with enough ball speed to optimize both. The problem is that it's very difficult to increase your drives' launch angle without also increasing the spin rate, so simply using a more lofted driver (say, switching from 10.5 degrees to 12) doesn't quite cut it because spin increases with club-head loft (the reason why you can

"The key ingredient to maximizing distance and accuracy is to attack the ball on the correct angle, and this angle changes depending if the ball is on the ground or if it's teed up."

back up shots hit into the green with your wedges but not your 3-iron). Your only way out of this problem is to optimize your angle of attack, and since angle of attack is part of your swing, it's something you can change—if you know how.

Here's how TrackMan™ inventor, Fredrik Tuxen, Ph.D., describes the effect of finding the correct angle of attack on your tee ball:

"If you have 90 mph of clubhead speed with an attack angle of minus 5 degrees (hitting down on the ball), your optimal launch angle and spin rate is around 10 degrees and 3,100 rpm. On the other hand, if your attack angle is plus 5 degrees (hitting up on the ball) with the same clubhead speed, your optimal launch angle and spin rate change to 16 degrees and 2,200 rpm."

And here's the big deal:

"This second combination will carry the ball almost 30 yards farther than the first."

The swing you use when the ball is on the ground won't work with your driver.

ALTERING YOUR ATTACK

To maximize your drives you need to hit the ball on an upswing, because this increases your launch angle without adding clubhead loft. You'll also produce less spin while increasing the force with which you hit the ball. It's also important to combine an ascending angle of attack with a path that moves the club right of the target through impact.

DESCENDING HIT
When you hit down on the ball, even as little as 5 degrees, you have virtually no chance with a standard-issue driver to achieve the optimal launch angle and spin rate. In fact, hitting down on the ball like this can cost you up to 30 yards of distance with a 90-mph swing.

FLAT HIT
It's logical to assume that the clubhead travels parallel to the ground through contact. However, striking the ball this way robs your drives of extra yards. Research shows that a flat hit generates 14 fewer yards from a 90-mph swing than one that strikes the ball on the upswing.

ASCENDING HIT
TrackMan™ research shows decisively that if you hit up on the ball by 4 to 6 degrees, you'll hit longer drives with less spin—without any increase in your swing speed. This ascending path creates the optimal launch because it increases club-to-ball energy transfer.

HOW TO CREATE AN ASCENDING ANGLE OF ATTACK

Your goal then is to *ascend* into the ball with a driver. Here are a few swing adjustments for you to try on for size—some combination of which will likely do the trick. Keep in mind that you probably won't need them all, but I recommend you experiment with each until you identify the ones that maximize your launch characteristics.

1 AIM RIGHT
Align your body and clubshaft angle to the right of your target. This will automatically help you swing more inside-to-out—a natural way to ascend into the ball. Make sure to aim your clubface at the target.

2 TAKE A STRONGER HOLD
Use a stronger grip by rotating your hands clockwise on the handle. A more closed face helps protect against heel contact.

3 LEAN THE SHAFT
Tilt the shaft of your driver slightly away from the target at address by pointing the butt of your club at your zipper.

4 GET CLOSER
The more forward you tee the ball, the more likely you'll address it off the toe. Stand closer to the ball to align it with the center of your clubface.

5 TEE HIGH & STAND WIDE
Tee the ball higher and move it forward in your stance. Then, move your right foot six inches wider. This naturally tilts your spine away from the target so you can hit up on the ball.

6

CHOOSE A HIGH TARGET
Pick a high point on the horizon and visualize the ball flying over it. If there's a cloud, hit up and into it to encourage an ascending strike.

AIM HERE

7

DROP BACK
Drop your right foot back away from the target line in a closed position, then adjust your shoulders to your heel line. This will encourage an inside-out swing. It's critical that you use your heels as your baseline and not your toes.

8

STOP THE BLOCK
As you power through impact, rotate your forearms in the direction of your swing (i.e., inside-out and up). Blocked forearm rotation doesn't match well with an inside-out, ascending swing.

9

DON'T GET STEEP
Allow the shaft to shallow out so it's more horizontal to the ground during the downswing. Keep your right elbow lower than your left as long as possible. This will make you feel like you're aligning to the right of your target, but trust it.

10

GET FIT
See your fitter when you successfully change your angle of attack—you'll need a less lofted driver to keep spin under control (and consult Chapter 10).

11

MAKE AN ASCENDING PRACTICE SWING
Take a rehearsal swing while saying to yourself, "Hit up on the ball."

"Hit up on the ball!"

12

MAINTAIN POSTURE
Caution: Swinging up on the ball doesn't mean "pulling up" on the ball. Keep your spine angle intact through impact.

NO!

Next Steps:
Swing with Both Eyes

In addition to the adjustments listed on the previous pages, I strongly recommend making the following changes based on a problem so widespread that it ruins the driving game at every skill level (including professionals). I call it the Cyclops Syndrome.

Cyclops is a monster from Greek mythology with only one eye, a condition that eventually spelled his doom. I call the problem the Cyclops Syndrome because of the fact that when you reach your full coil at the top of your backswing you can only see the ball out of your left eye, and when you go from a two-eyed fix on an object (like you have at address) to a one-eyed fix (like you get at the top), the ball appears to move. (Yes, it moves. Prove it to yourself with the test at right.) This problem is especially rampant among golfers with big noses, minimum flexibility, those who wear glasses and players with long, loopy swings.

The majority of players react to the ball appearing to have moved by spinning their shoulders immediately as they start their downswing. This is the primary cause of an over-the-top swing, with your club cutting across the ball at impact instead of powering through it. Not only will this produce a wicked slice nine times out of 10, it makes it extremely difficult to maintain the correct swing plane and angle of attack with your driver.

So the average golfer is stuck—establish a strong coil with a long swing and lose two-eyed vision and

CYCLOPS TEST
Extend your right arm in front of you with your index finger pointing up. Look at your finger with both eyes then quickly close one eye and then the other. Your finger will appear to move as you alternate.

cut across the ball, or refrain from coiling and suffer an embarrassing lack of distance.

The takeaway here is that it can't be cured via swing mechanics because it's caused by a visual problem. I learned a long time ago to fix the cause and not the effect. Now that you know the cause of your driver woes, here's the fix [*Drill, right*].

"A high positive attack angle with your driver gives you the potential to achieve long carry and total distance limited only by your clubhead speed. But in order to take advantage of this potential, you still need to hit the ball in the center of the clubface, align your clubhead path and clubface angle toward the target, and finally use the proper clubhead design, loft, and shaft in combination with the ball you play."

—*Fredrik Tuxen, Ph.D., TrackMan™ inventor*

DRILL

Swing with One Eye

The key is to become accustomed to losing sight of the ball with your right eye and utilizing your left eye to see the ball at the top of your backswing. Once you develop this ability you'll be able to make a much fuller backswing and swing down to impact on plane while delivering a more ascending blow.

1. Put an eye patch over your right eye or simply close your right eye. If you do the latter, be sure not to cheat. You're now a golfing Cyclops.

2. Swing back to the top like normal. When you get to the top you won't be able to see the ball with both eyes because your right-eye vision is blocked by your nose. Here's where most golfers turn their head to re-establish two-eyed vision, and they do it while also turning their shoulders and their chest back toward the target. This is why most golfers trying to hit "the big one" off the tee come over the top (it can just as easily happen with your irons).

3. Hit twenty balls with your driver, keeping your right eye closed. Make a full turn away from the ball each time, making sure you keep your left eye focused on the ball.

4. Take the patch off or open your right eye and try to replicate the same swing with a full turn. You should soon feel comfortable using your left eye during your swing.

NO!

Since my shoulders haven't turned much I could still see the ball with both eyes if I didn't have the patch on. After a few shots like this I'll learn to rely on my left eye.

YES!

Once you train yourself to see with only one eye you won't feel the need to spin your shoulders from the top of your backswing.

THE TWO-SWING SYSTEM

To better understand the ball-on-a-tee swing (the one you use with your driver) you need to first understand the ball-on-the-ground swing. If your goal is to have the club path and clubface looking at the target at impact (vertical D-Plane from Chapter 1) then your swing needs to be not only descending but also outside-to-in with all clubs except the driver.

You'll hit the ball straight with an iron even though you swing left because you're hitting down on the ball. In fact, it's the outside-in direction coupled with a descending strike that allows a higher percentage of square hits. When you abide by the laws of physics and geometry probability is your friend. The geometry changes when you put the driver in your hands. You maximize ball flight with the driver using a positive or ascending angle of attack. In other words, you catch the ball on the upswing with the driver.

YOUR GOAL
Hit up on your driver and down on everything else, but to do this correctly you need two swing paths: A driver swing that ascends inside-out, and a descending outside-in swing for everything else.

BALL-ON-GROUND SWING
Point your clubface at the target, but set the vertical component of your plane to the left. This will make it easier to square the path and face at impact.

BALL-ON-GROUND SWING

STEEP & OUT-TO-IN: To hit the ball straight with an iron, swing to the left of your target while hitting down on the ball.

BALL-ON-TEE SWING
Set the vertical component of your plane to the right of your target at address to promote the correct inside-out swing.

A Revolutionary Concept

Golf is a game of probabilities, and players who have mastered the two-swing concept are better as the universe of attempts increases. Note that it's not that you can't hit good shots with your driver using a descending blow. Many tour players with high swing speeds do, but over time you satisfy the laws of impact more often by delivering an upward blow from the inside. Once you understand the concept of the two swings you can see why treating every club in your bag with the same setup and swing is a step on the road to failure. ●

5 THINGS TO TAKE FROM THIS CHAPTER

1 If you never mix good iron days with good driver days then you're using only one swing.

2 You can change your angle of attack from negative to positive by tweaking your setup and swing.

3 TrackMan™ studies indicate that you hit up on the ball with an inside-out swing for max distance and accuracy with a driver, and do the opposite for irons. This mandates the need for two swings.

4 The difference in angle of attack between your driver and your other clubs is based on the fact that you tee the ball up with your driver and play everything else from the ground.

5 You'll have trouble creating a positive angle of attack if you don't learn to trust seeing the ball with your left eye only at the top of your backswing.

BALL-ON-TEE SWING

SHALLOW & IN-TO-OUT: To hit the ball straight with your driver, swing to the right of your target while hitting up on the ball.

3-POST/LOW-TRACK DRIVER
RICKIE FOWLER

His shoulder-shaft downswing slot is
one of the Tour's most dynamic moves

Rickie Fowler can afford all of the oversized caps he wants after a brilliant rookie PGA Tour campaign in 2010. He's a bit of a throwback in that he doesn't worry much about positions or how his swing looks. His only concern is what's happening at impact. If that's good, then it's all good. That isn't to say he's reckless. In fact, a quick look at his swing shows that he does a lot of the things that more traditional players do. It's a perfect blend of fundamentals and personal style.

Rickie stands tall with a straight back (no bulges or curves) and a slight tilt from his hips. He looks like he can pounce in any direction with his weight evenly balanced.

Fowler is a natural low-track player [*see Chapter 3*]. You can see him hit his track early [*Frame 3*], but as he sets the club he rises to the right-arm plane [*Frame 5*], and then he just about gets to the shoulder plane at the top [*Frame 6*]. This happens in almost every swing—you elevate up at least one plane after you fold your right arm.

Suddenly, Fowler clears his left side from the ground up and with such speed that his club drops all the way back down to the shaft plane [*Frame 8*]. You can tell that this is his natural track by the fact that he maintains his spine angle and distance from the ball. His club exits on a higher plane [*Frame 13*] because of his severe inside-out delivery. Awesome.

Just about every golfer elevates up at least one plane because of the folding action of the right arm.

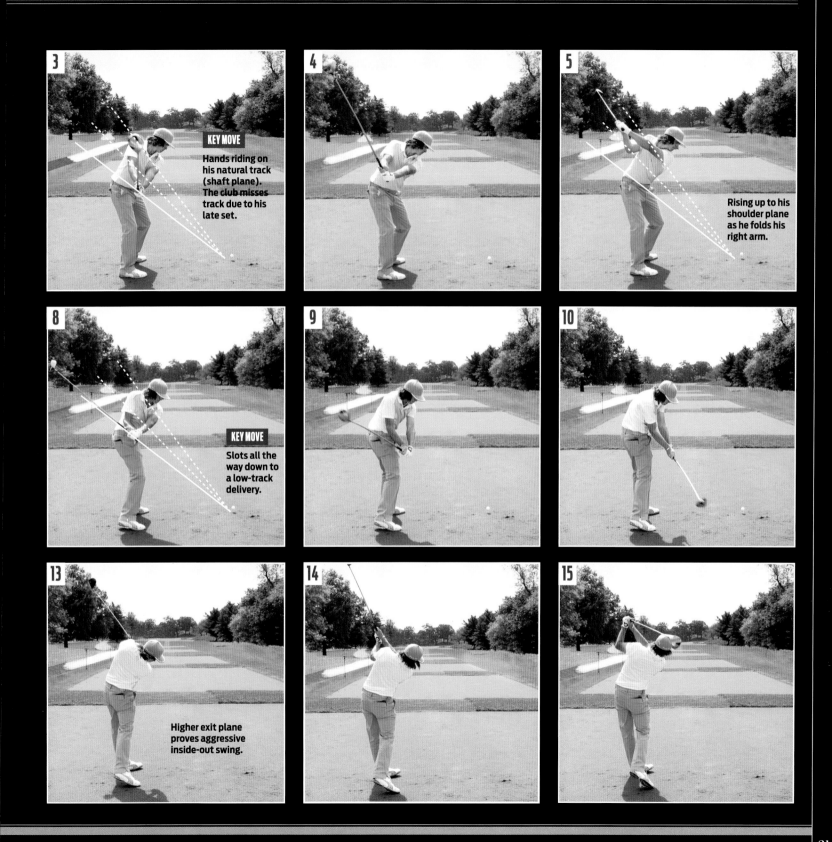

3

KEY MOVE

Hands riding on his natural track (shaft plane). The club misses track due to his late set.

4

5

Rising up to his shoulder plane as he folds his right arm.

8

KEY MOVE

Slots all the way down to a low-track delivery.

9

10

13

Higher exit plane proves aggressive inside-out swing.

14

15

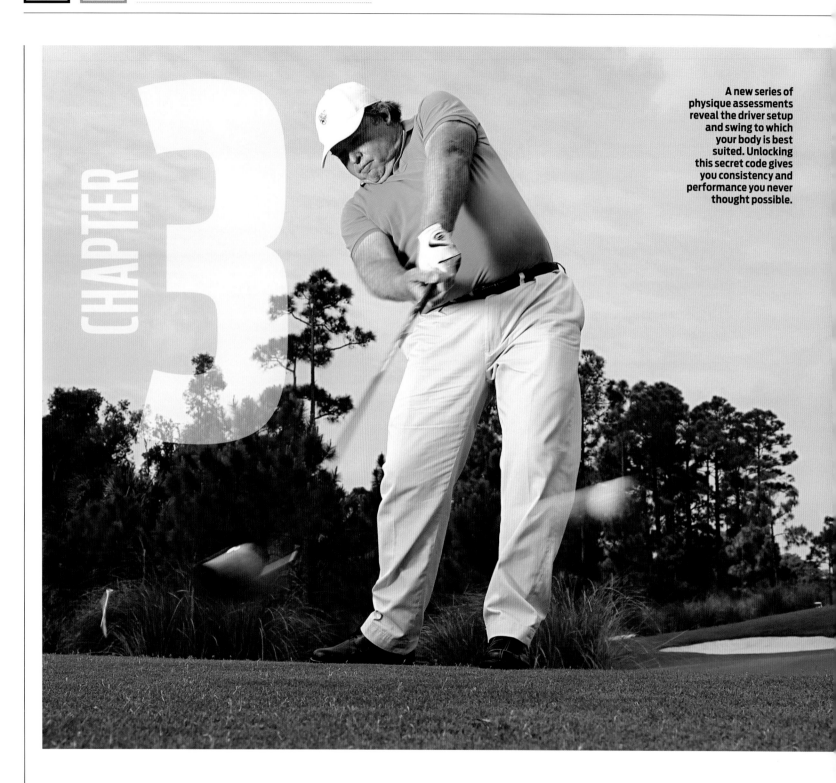

CHAPTER

A new series of physique assessments reveal the driver setup and swing to which your body is best suited. Unlocking this secret code gives you consistency and performance you never thought possible.

HOW TO FIND *YOUR* BEST
SETUP &
SWING

You don't choose your swing. *It chooses you.*
Find out what it has selected with a series of
tests that exposes—for the first time—your
most dynamic and efficient motion.

By **MIKE ADAMS**
Hamilton Farm G.C.
Gladstone, N.J.

THE GOLF SWING IS THE MOST analyzed and discussed athletic motion in existence. Anyone who has ever taught or played the game has had a preconceived idea—right or wrong—of how the club should be swung. The multitude of theories over the years has produced enormous confusion on the proper way to set up and to move the club back and through to produce desired results. I've dedicated all of my 30-plus years of teaching to separating swing facts from swing fiction, and righting popular misconceptions that make it difficult for players at any level to succeed. The purpose of this chapter is to eliminate any confusion you may have about your own swing, and set you on a well-defined path to longer and straighter shots.

The problem lies in the fact that 99 percent of the instruction you read in books and magazines, see on TV or receive from your coach is correct. It's just that much of it doesn't apply to you because it's too general to match your specific needs. The secret to success is finding and listening to the percentage that does.

Form always follows function, and the function of your swing is to consistently deliver the clubhead to the back of the ball on the desired path within the desired plane, catching it in the center of the sweet spot with the clubface square to the target and the whole system moving at maximum velocity. As far as the resulting form is concerned, it's often lost because the majority of coaches over-emphasize a preferred technique or style, drilling on hard-set positions and moves to which everyone must adapt, and they do this despite the fact that golfers come in unique sizes and shapes and with very different abilities and desires. Your form can't be dictated to you. I make the case that you dictate form. Doesn't it make sense that your anatomy would have something to do with how you should swing the club? It makes perfect sense, otherwise you're putting the proverbial square peg into the round hole, setting in motion an ineffective chain of events that, truthfully, will keep your game at the same level it's languishing at right now and potentially cause you an injury.

I first broached the subject of using body type as a way to determine swing shape in 1998 with fellow Top 100 Teachers Jim Suttie and T.J. Tomasi in *The LAWs of the Golf Swing*, a popular book that prescribed a swing system based on whether your build was best suited for you to swing like a Leverage, Arc or Width player. Following *LAWs*, I continued to research the shape/swing dynamic, and ultimately developed a series of tests (the ones you'll take in this chapter) that nails your golf body type like never before to help you determine not only the shape of your swing, but also how to set up for it, power it, and make it consistent. The tests are very simple—no preparation needed—and take but seconds to complete. Once you run through them, however, the information gained will change your golfing life for the good for years on end.

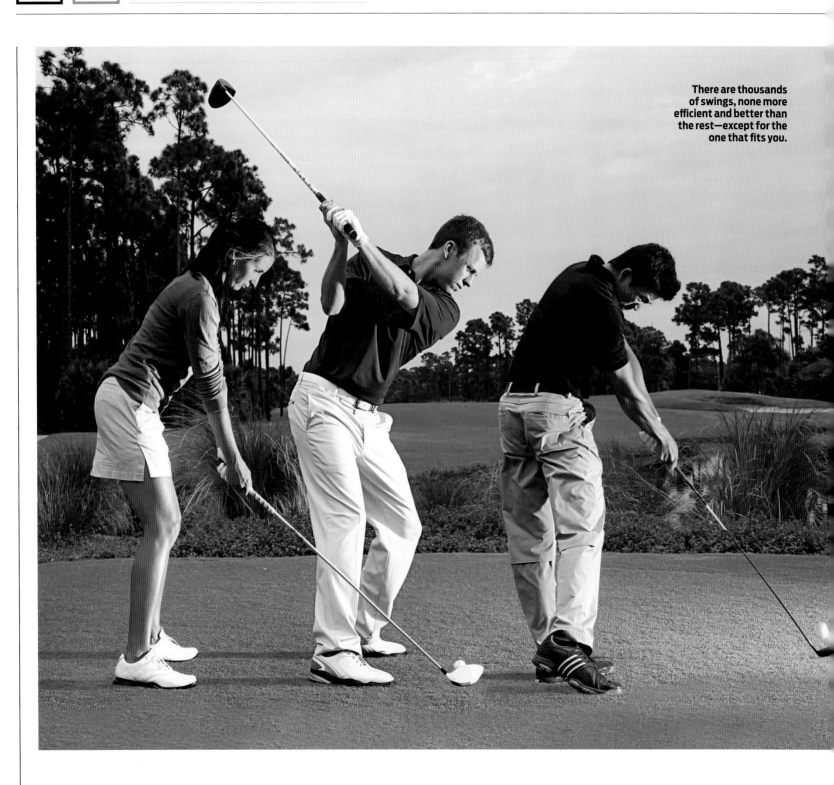

There are thousands of swings, none more efficient and better than the rest—except for the one that fits you.

FINDING YOUR BEST SWING: TEST BY TEST

I n this chapter you'll perform four simple tests, and with the completion of each one you'll learn more and more about the best way for you to take your driver—any club for that matter—and swing it back and up, then down and through the ball. A lot of the information you'll discover also relates to the material in the next chapter, the authors of which help expand on your best swing type by refining its key segments and the moves required to make its overall motion smooth and consistent. As we proceed, you're going to come across many new terms. Most of these—like tracking, slotting and delivering—have long histories within instruction circles. This book, however, represents the first time they've been packaged together as a readable road map for the amateur player.

The basic plan for the testing/discovery phase for unlocking your driver swing code is thus:

1. Take an **Arm Length Test** to determine if the overall motion of your swing should be rotary or lateral.

2. Take an **Elbow Hinge Test** to determine the ideal path on which you should swing your driver (all clubs, really) back and, in most cases, the plane on which you should deliver the club into the ball, regardless if your motion is rotary or lateral.

3. Take a **Lower-Body Action Test** to determine the pivot action that best suits you and your swing.

4. Take a **Hip Speed Test** to inform you of the speed of your pivot, and how to adjust your setup to exploit your rotational speed for maximum distance and direction.

Together, the tests reveal the biomechanically and anatomically most dynamic and efficient way you should swing your driver. Moreover, they reveal your most natural athletic motion so that you can make swings without manipu-

---

Driver Swing Code Book

Mark the boxes once you complete each test, and place a check next to your results so you can refer to your code when presented with the different swing options in this chapter and the next.

❏ **Arm Length:** ___ +/- 4" of height (*rotary swing*) ___ > 4" of height (*lateral swing*)

❏ **Elbow Hinge:** ___ Below shoulder (*low track*) ___ At shoulder (*mid track*)
___ Above shoulder (*high track*)

❏ **Body Action:** ___ Left leg (*1-post*) ___ Right leg (*2-post*)
___ Pelvis (*center post*) ___ 3-post

❏ **Hip Speed:** ___ Slow ___ Medium ___ Fast

"Together, the tests reveal the biomechanically and anatomically most dynamic and efficient way you should swing your driver."

lation or placing undue stress on your muscles and joints. As soon as you complete these tests, you'll know more about the swing that best fits your makeup than 99 percent of the golfers out there, and will have successfully sifted through the mountain of confusing and contradicting swing instruction so that you can focus on the small section that applies only to you. With your goal so clearly defined your improvement will soar exponentially as you practice and groove your technique. Basically, you'll be driving the ball better very soon.

SWING CODE GLOSSARY

Below are the key terms you'll need to become familiar with as you read this chapter (and the next) to fully unlock your driver swing code.

Rotary swing: Movement back and through the ball dominated predominantly by rotation.

Lateral swing: A swing that, because of a high-hands position at the top of the backswing, requires a substantial, lateral lower-body shift at the start of the downswing to position the club on the proper delivery plane.

Post: The axis of your rotation. You can rotate around one, two or even three posts.

Anchor: The act of establishing your weight over a post.

Track: The plane and path your clubhead travels on during your backswing.

Top of track: The position of the clubhead at the top of your backswing.

Slot: Downswing plane between the top of the track and the delivery plane.

Slotting: The shifting in the plane of the shaft and clubhead from the top of the track to the delivery plane.

Delivery plane: The downswing plane of the clubhead and shaft as they approach the ball.

Delivery motor: The body mass (typically the shoulders, torso or hips) that powers the club on the delivery plane and through impact. Ideally the delivery motor and plane match (i.e., shoulders deliver the club on the shoulder plane, torso delivers the club on the right-arm plane and hips deliver the club on the shaft plane).

STEP 1: DECODE YOUR SWING TYPE

Take the test below to determine the main design of your swing.

TEST: Arm Length

Tools required: Measuring tape.
What the results tell you: Whether you should use a rotary swing or a lateral swing.
How to do it: Stand erect with your arms spread straight out and your palms open. Have a friend measure the distance from fingertips to fingertips.

Decoding the Results

Arm length determines your best hand position at the top, and this hand position determines how you bring the club back. As such, this simple test shows you the base action of your swing.

If your fingertip-to-fingertip length is +/- 4" of your height, you're built to swing the club utilizing a rotary motion. The length of your arms naturally sets your hands at the top position within a range where you can effectively bring them back down on the correct plane simply by turning your body.

If your fingertip-to-fingertip length is *more than 4" longer* than your height, then you're built to use a lateral swing. Your extra arm length means that your most natural hand position at the top of your backswing is above your shoulder. With your hands positioned so high, you'll need a lateral shift at the start of your downswing to drop them onto an acceptable delivery plane.

Arm length determines your fundamental swing action.

A lateral swing is basically the 2-plane swing model made famous by Jim Hardy in his *Plane Truth for Golfers* books and schools, and a rotary swing is Hardy's 1-plane model. You'll learn about these motions in more detail in the next chapter. For now, mark your Code Book and proceed with the next test.

NOTE: The "ideal" arm length measurement in this test above is one that matches your height right on the button. This type of symmetry sets you up for a perfect address without your having to make any adjustments.

If, however, your arms are slightly longer than—yet within 4" of—your height, pull your shoulders back at address. This will "shorten" your arms so that you don't create too flat a lie angle with you driver. If you fall into the shorter arms category, round your shoulders forward at address, effectively increasing their length so you won't have to stand so close to the ball. Increasing your knee flex also will help you hit the ball more solidly if you tested out for shorter arms.

TALE OF THE ARM-LENGTH TAPE

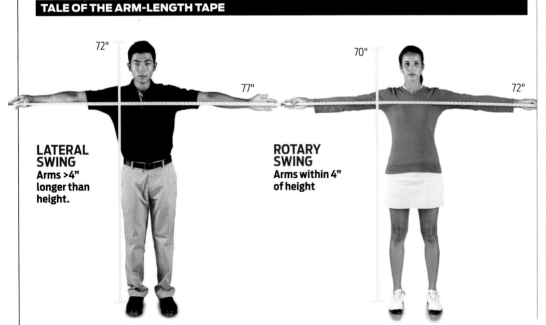

72"
77"
LATERAL SWING
Arms >4" longer than height.

70"
72"
ROTARY SWING
Arms within 4" of height

CHART YOUR PROGRESS

- ☑ **Arm Length Test** *(rotary or lateral swing)*
- ❏ **Elbow Hinge Test** *(best clubhead path)*
- ❏ **Lower-Body Action Test** *(best pivot type)*
- ❏ **Hip Speed Test** *(best pivot rate)*

STEP 2: DECODE YOUR TRACK

Take the test below to determine your ideal backswing (and potentially downswing) clubhead path.

TEST: Elbow Hinge

Tools required: None.

What the results tell you: Whether you're a low-track, mid-track or high-track golfer.

How to do it: Stand tall and point your right thumb out like a hitchhiker. Set your right elbow against your rib cage just in front of the side seam on your shirt and fold your upper arm up without pulling you elbow off your rib cage. Check where your thumb points in relation to your right shoulder.

Decoding the Results

The Elbow Test exposes the difference (if any) between the length of your upper arm and the length of your forearm. This is important because as you swing your right elbow back in your takeaway, a longer right forearm (compared to your upper arm) will obviously "track" the clubhead higher relative to your elbow. The opposite is true if your forearm is shorter than your upper arm. Basically, the Elbow Hinge Test defines your ideal backswing plane.

If your thumb points *below* the top of your shoulder then you're a low-track golfer. Your ideal backswing clubhead path is defined by the plane that the shaft of your driver (any club, really) sits on at address (shaft plane).

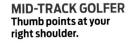

Thumb your way to a better swing.

If your thumb points *even* with the top of your shoulder then you're a mid-track golfer. Your ideal backswing clubhead path is defined by the plane that extends from the target line (base line of the plane at the ball) through the tip of your right elbow at address (right-arm plane).

If your thumb points *above* the top of your shoulder then you're a high-track golfer. Your ideal backswing clubhead path is defined by the plane from the target line through the right shoulder at address (shoulder plane).

NOTE: The Elbow Test describes your best backswing clubhead path. It's also a strong indicator of your best delivery plane. You'll nail this section of your swing with E.A. Tischler in the next chapter, but for now, consider the results of the Elbow Test as your most efficient swing plane both back and through.

> **"Basically, the Elbow Hinge Test defines your ideal backswing—and potentially downswing—plane."**

HOW TO DECODE YOUR IDEAL CLUBHEAD PATH

LOW-TRACK GOLFER
Thumb points below your right shoulder.

MID-TRACK GOLFER
Thumb points at your right shoulder.

HIGH-TRACK GOLFER
Thumb points above your right shoulder.

CHART YOUR PROGRESS
- ☑ **Arm Length Test** *(rotary or lateral swing)*
- ☑ **Elbow Hinge Test** *(best clubhead path)*
- ❏ **Lower-Body Action Test** *(best pivot type)*
- ❏ **Hip Speed Test** *(best pivot rate)*

TRACKS IN ACTION

Your track (low, mid or high) represents your ideal backswing plane. It's also a strong indicator of your ideal delivery plane (you'll check for sure in the next chapter). In a perfect world you swing your club back on your track on your way to the top, and deliver it to the back to the ball on the same plane. This is called a **1-plane pure rotary swing** (you can think of it as track-to-track), and while you'll read about other ways to move your club in between your backswing and delivery track (by slotting your club above or below your natural plane, or by applying Jim Hardy's 2-plane method), minding your track from start to finish produces the most consistent contact and reduces the stress absorbed by your body when you swing to a very low level, keeping injuries or pain to a minimum.

It's important to note that the three tracks are equal—no one track is better than the rest. A low-track swing, for example, won't produce any more distance or accuracy than a high-track swing and vice-versa. It's a matter of what best fits your body.

Regardless of how you fine-tune your track based on the refinement tests presented by E.A. Tischler in the next chapter, missing your natural track as you swing the club back and to the top is Step 1 in a bad chain of events. Honestly, missing your track is actually difficult to do since a swinging club will naturally seek out its natural plane if you allow it to. To check it, however, make your backswing with a mirror to your immediate right and stop your motion when the club is parallel to the ground with

the butt of the grip pointing at your target line. If you tested out as a low-track swinger then the shaft should ride on the plane defined by the shaft angle at address; if you're a mid-track swinger then the shaft should track on the plane defined by your right arm at address; a high-track swinger should motion the shaft in-line with the plane defined by his or her shoulders at address [*photo, above*]. You can perform the same test to check your delivery position, stopping your swing when the shaft points the target line in your downswing.

Finding your natural track makes it easy to swing with a dynamic and efficient motion.

1: HIGH-TRACK SWINGER
Clubhead path defined by a plane line drawn from the target line up through the right shoulder socket (shoulder plane).

2: MID-TRACK SWINGER
Clubhead path defined by the plane the right arm sits on at address (line drawn from target line, or base, line, through the tip of right elbow). This is why the mid-track path is also referred to as the right-arm plane.

3: LOW-TRACK SWINGER
Clubhead path defined by plane the shaft sits on at address (line from ground up shaft), which is why the low-track path is also referred to as the shaft plane.

DEFINITIONS
Pure Rotary (Track-to-Track) Swing: Clubhead swings back on the golfer's natural plane and returns to the ball on the natural plane. Also a 1-plane motion.

Slotted Rotary Swing: Clubhead swings back on the golfer's natural plane and returns to the ball on a different plane. The shift to the second plane is called "slotting."

2-Plane Swing: Any swing other than a rotary-driven motion (requires a substantial lateral shift at the start of the downswing).

PURE ROTARY (TRACK-TO-TRACK) SWINGS ON TOUR

The backswing and downswing clubhead paths of some of the best drivers on Tour prove that hitting it consistently long and straight is easiest when you swing track-to-track.

RICKIE FOWLER
Track: **Low-to-low**

Swings back along his shaft plane and delivers the club to the ball along his shaft plane.

ERNIE ELS
Track: **Mid-to-mid**

Swings back along his right-arm plane and delivers the club along his right-arm plane.

MARTIN LAIRD
Track: **High-to-high**

Swings back along his shoulder plane and delivers the club along his shoulder plane.

SLOTTED ROTARY SWINGS ON TOUR

Swings that switch tracks aren't as efficient as those that don't, yet are nonetheless a real and viable option for many golfers (and you may be one of them). You'll learn if you're a candidate for slotting the club to a plane above or below your natural track in the next chapter. A lot of players utilize slot swings to draw and fade the ball. If you go back on a lower plane and come down on a higher plane you'll probably hit fades. Conversely, if you take the club back on a higher plane and swing it down on a lower plane you'll probably hit a draw.

BILL HAAS
Track: **High-to-mid**

Swings back along his shoulder plane and delivers the club along his right-arm plane.

MATT KUCHAR
Track: **Low-to-mid**

Swings back along his shaft plane and delivers the club along his right-arm plane.

PHIL MICKELSON
Track: **Mid-to-high**

Swings back along his right-arm plane and delivers the club along his shoulder plane.

FALLING OFF TRACK

Switching tracks is perfectly allowed as long as it fits your body. When it breaks the rules, trouble can and will happen if for the only reason that swinging off-track is not ideal and, therefore, prone to inconsistency. (Keep in mind that switching tracks by slotting the club is fine if and when you test for it, which you'll do with E.A. Tischler in the next chapter).

DROPPING FROM THE MIDDLE TRACK

EXHIBIT A: RORY McILROY
Elbow Test result:
Mid-track (right thumb even with right shoulder)
Typical swing:
Mid-track to low-track

McIlroy tests out as a mid-track swinger, but drops down to the low-track (hip) delivery plane for his trademark draw.

Notice how McIlroy hits his natural right-arm plane with ease as he swings back, but as he comes down from the top, his aggressive torso and hip move drop the club all the way down to the shaft plane. In other words, he delivers the club below his natural track. McIlroy often makes up for it with sheer athleticism (see 2011 U.S. Open) and, let's be honest, youth, but over time this will cause a problem with inconsistency and a tendency to hit blocks and wrap hooks, which currently are his big misses (see 10th hole, final round of 2011 Masters).

DROPPING FROM THE HIGH TRACK

EXHIBIT B: DUSTIN JOHNSON
Elbow Test result:
High-track (right thumb above with right shoulder)
Typical swing:
High-track to mid-track

Johnson is a high-track golfer, but misses his track in the delivery, making him long but inaccurate off the tee.

Dustin Johnson is a natural high-track player with one of the most dynamic and explosive swings in the game. He swings the club back perfectly on his shoulder plane. On the way down, however, he tucks his right arm into his side, shutting the clubface and dropping the club to his right-arm plane. He delivers the club to the ball below his natural track, causing his ball striking to be much more inconsistent than it ever should be. Check the sequence on page 88 to see how Johnson compensates for such a strong downward slot.

STEP 3: DECODING YOUR LOWER BODY ACTION

Take the test below to determine how you should pivot and transfer your weight as you swing both back and through for optimal contact.

TEST: Lower-Body Action

Tools required: Any club.

What the results tell you: Whether you're a 1-post, 2-post (possibly 3-post), or a center-post golfer.

How to do it: Place the shaft of any club across the top of both thighs with your feet hip-width apart and slightly flared. Next, simply rotate your hips back making sure the shaft stays in contact with your thighs.

Decoding the Results

Whether you know it or not your lower body has its own way of moving the most dynamically and efficiently. This goes for everything you do that involves lower-body rotation, like hitting a baseball, swinging a tennis racquet and, of course, hitting your driver and irons.

If your weight *shifts to your left leg* when you rotate your hips to the back, you're a 1-post golfer. You're naturally structured to anchor your weight over your left leg and pivot around it from start to finish in any athletic motion.

If your weight *shifts to your right leg* when you rotate your hips to the right, you're a 2-post golfer. You're structured to pivot around your right leg as you load up in your backswing and pivot around your left leg in your forward-swing.

If your weight *doesn't feel like it's favoring one leg or the other* when you rotate your hips to the right, you're a center-post golfer. You're naturally structured to anchor your weight over the your pelvis and rotate around your body's center from start to finish.

The Lower-Body Action Test shows that there are three different turns (there's actually a fourth—see page 45), three different weight shifts, and three equally dynamic and efficient ways to move your lower body when you swing. If you stray from your natural lower-body action, you'll have difficulty maintaining your track and delivering the club to the ball with consistency and with sufficient swing speed.

CHART YOUR PROGRESS
- ☑ **Arm Length Test** *(rotary or lateral swing)*
- ☑ **Elbow Hinge Test** *(best clubhead path)*
- ☑ **Lower-Body Action Test** *(best pivot type)*
- ☐ **Hip Speed Test** *(best pivot rate)*

HOW TO DECODE YOUR PIVOT

1-POST GOLFER
Rotates around the left leg both on the backswing and forward-swing.

2-POST GOLFER
Rotates back on the right leg and rotates forward on the left leg.

CENTER-POST GOLFER
Rotates around pelvis in a centered action both back and through.

FLEX
Bending your left knee as you swing to the top helps you anchor weight where you need it in a 1-post swing.

STRAIGHTEN
Post your left leg as you swing into impact. This causes your spine to straighten as well and create a wall your clubhead can zip past with max acceleration.

FLARE
Flaring your left foot at address encourages you to flex your left knee and facilitates moving further left in your downswing to appropriately slot the club.

1-POST LOWER-BODY ACTION

The 1-post rotation style is the lower-body motion taught by renowned instructors Sean Foley (Tiger Woods' coach), Mike Bennett and Andy Plummer (*Stack & Tilt* system), and Mac O'Grady (*Lean and Load* method). I teach it when it's a natural fit for the student (as determined by the Lower-Body Action test), as does E.A. Tischler (who applies the term "front anchor" as you'll read about in the next chapter).

In you tested out for the 1-post action, set your right foot square to your target line and flare out your left at address (you'll determine the amount of flare on page 48). Squaring your right foot causes your right leg to straighten, helping you maintain weight over your left leg. Flaring your left foot encourages your left knee to flex in the direction of your left foot. It also allows your hips to move forward on your downswing so that you're able to drop the club down from your shoulder plane—which everyone hits after the right arm folds following the takeaway—and onto your natural track. It's also a good idea to purposely stack your weight over your left leg before you begin your swing.

If you test out as a 1-poster, consult E.A. Tischler's advice in Chapter 4. Also, books by Bennett & Plummer and Mac O'Grady are worth your time. In the meantime, a few bullet points:

1) As flex your left knee in your backswing you should feel your spine lean toward the target and your shoulders turn on an incline.

2) You should also feel like everything is rotating around your left leg, taking the club deep around your body.

3) Clear your left hip at the start of your downswing and allow your left leg to straighten. Clearing delivers the club correctly on track. Straightening your leg causes your spine to do likewise, causing the club to accelerate to max speed.

2-POST LOWER-BODY ACTION

In a 2-post swing your right hip turns back over your right heel to establish your backswing pivot point (post No. 1). Once this right-side pivot point is established, you're able to around it as you swing to the top. As you start back down, maintain this pivot point until your left hip turns back over your left heel, at which time you establish your downswing pivot point (post No. 2). To do this correctly, imagine a wall behind your right hip at the start of your downswing. Your right cheek should maintain contact with the wall until you establish your second post. This creates a very noticeable bow-legged look in most 2-posters. Once the left leg post is established, turn your right side around your left hip and eventually past it.

POST 1
Your right leg is your backswing pivot point.

POST 2
Your left leg is your downswing pivot point.

CENTER-POST LOWER BODY ACTION

As a center rotater you will rotate back and through around you pelvis (use your belt buckle as your guide). Percy Boomer's legendary image of "turning in a barrel" best describes how your lower body should feel as you rotate around a centered post. Better yet, think of it this way: Your right hip turns behind on your backswing you on your backswing and your left hip turns behind you and on your downswing.

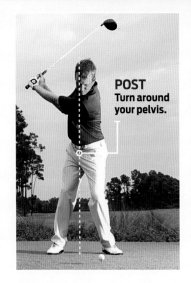

POST
Turn around your pelvis.

POST
In a center-post rotation, simply think of turning in a barrel.

Lateral hips

As a lateral player you need a wider stance to encourage your hips to move laterally, not rotationally. Set your right foot square and your left foot open to the target line. The square right foot causes your right leg to straighten during your backswing. This encouraged your right hip to sit higher than your left at the top, setting up the downswing fall. From here slide your hips forward until you feel your left hip reach your left foot, at which time your left hip takes over by rotating back over your left heel with the ret of your body turning around your left leg. Likely in the past you've been told not to slide your hips on your downswing, but if you tested out to be a 2-plane golfer in the Lower-Body Action Test then you need this lateral shift to slot the club onto your natural delivery plane.

3-POST TEST

If you're a rotary 2-post golfer, there's a test to determine if you're a 3-poster. Sit on a chair with your knees hip-width apart, set a club across the top of your shoulders and hold it in place by crossing your arms across your chest. Next, bend forward from your hips until your elbows are almost touching your thighs [photo, below left]. From this position, turn your chest and shoulders as far to the right as possible without moving your head or your spine. If the shaft turns beyond your left knee then you're a 3-post golfer who should rotate first around your spine, around your right hip on your backswing, and finally around your left hip on the downswing. If you can't turn far enough to get the shaft past your left knee then you're a 2-post golfer. A 2-post golfer, again, rotates around their right leg on the backswing and their left leg on the downswing, helping to create force without maximum flexibility.

STEP 4: DECODING YOUR PIVOT SPEED

Now that you know how you pivot, take the test at right to discover you how fast this pivot should take place, and how to adjust your setup to exploit your rotation for max yards.

TEST: Hip Speed
Tools required: Boxing punch mitt (a sofa cushion or headcover works, too).
What the results tell you: Everything you must change in your setup to accommodate your personal rate of rotation.
How to do it: Take your address position without a club with your right arm hanging freely. Have a friend stand opposite you and set a boxing puncher's mitt (or carefully held sofa cushion) right where your right hand would be at impact. Set your right palm against the mitt or cushion, swing your arm back like you would in a golf swing and then slap the mitt or cushion with your palm with your lower body delivering the hand to impact. Mimic your full swing as much as possible and don't hold back.

RATE OF RETURN
The Hip Speed Test tells you how fast you should rotate and adjust your setup to make the most of it.

Decoding the Results

Your hip and right foot position at impact tells you how fast you turn in your golf swing. While hip speed by itself doesn't prescribe a "best swing" for you, it has a serious effect on the way you set up at address to best utilize the natural speed of your personal rate of rotation.

If your hips are directly facing the target and your right heel is completely off the ground, you have fast hips.

If your hips have turned about 45° past the mitt or cushion your right heel is partially elevated off the ground, you have medium-speed hips.

If your hips have turned only slightly toward the target and your right heel is still on the ground, you have slow hips.

Is it better to have fast hips, slow hips or medium-speed hips? They're all good. Adam Scott only has medium-speed and Kenny Perry has slow hips yet both can knock the ball 300 yards any time they want because they match their hip speed with the necessary setup adjustments to maximize their swings [see Adam's sequence, page 102]. Don't cheat and be something you're not.

> **"Hip speed has a serious effect on the way you set up at address to best utilize the natural speed of your personal rate of rotation."**

CHART YOUR PROGRESS

- ☑ **Arm Length Test** *(rotary or lateral swing)*
- ☑ **Elbow Hinge Test** *(best clubhead path)*
- ☑ **Lower-Body Action Test** *(best pivot type)*
- ☑ **Hip Speed Test** *(best pivot rate)*

SLOW
Hips slightly open to target, right heel on ground.

MEDIUM
Hips 45 degrees open to target, left heel slightly up.

FAST
Hips facing target, right heel all the way up.

IMPORTANT NOTES ON THE TESTS

As you learn more about tracking, slotting and 1- and 2-plane swings in the next chapter, you'll soon realize that while swinging track-to-track is your most ideal option, chest thickness and desired shot shape will help you determine which combination of backswing tracks and downswing delivery planes you'll put to use.

A thicker chest typically forces an earlier shoulder turn (because your left arms almost immediately runs into your torso as you start the club back), and the earlier shoulder turn forces you to access a lower plane during your takeaway.

Slotting to a lower delivery plane from your natural backswing plane typically results in a draw. If this is the shot shape you prefer, then you'll utilize a lower track than natural coming down.

Slotting to a higher delivery plane from your natural backswing plane typically results in a fade. If this is the shot shape you prefer, then you'll utilize a higher track than natural coming down.

NOTE: If you look at any swing sequence of any player (like the nine featured between the chapters in this book) you'll that notice most of them end up at or near the shoulder plane at the top of the backswing (also known as top of the track—see Chapter 4). This is because **the folding action in your right elbow following your arm swing and initial turn away from the ball elevates the club to the shoulder plane.** That's why it's important to look at track when the shaft is parallel to the ground—before the right-arm has elevated the club.

PUTTNG YOUR BEST SWING TOGETHER

NOTE: Keep in mind that there's much more to discover about your new motion in the next chapter. E.A. Tischler will help you refine each of the swing parameters you tested for to help you further nail your motion, while teaching legends Jim Hardy and Jim McLean explain the more detailed workings of 1- and 2-plane motions, and the fine art of slotting, respectively.

B ased on how you tested for swing type (rotary or lateral), swing track (low, mid or high), rotation (1-post, 2-post, center-post or 3-post) and hip speed (slow, medium or fast), there are hard and fast rules you need to adhere to at address and some general rules to apply to your motion to hit the consistently successful drives. I've designed each of these adjustments to maximize every swing combination possible, from a rotary/low-track/1-post/slow-hips position through lateral/high-track/3-post/fast-hips position. Here are the 7 new rules for your swing.

1. Posture

Stand erect and place your hands on your thighs. Next, bend forward from your hip sockets while simultaneously sliding your hands down your legs [*photos, below*]. Stop when your fingers touch your knees. Relax your knees and you should feel

like you're in a balanced, athletic position. If you dropped a plumb line down from the top of your spine it would run past the tips of your elbows, tips of your knees and the balls of your feet. The beauty of this routine is that it establishes your most dynamic position for creating and delivering force, and guarantees that your arms and club will stay in front of you throughout (i.e., swinging between your shoulders).

KEY ADJUSTMENTS

Rotary swing—None. The setup procedure above should set your clubshaft and spine at right angles, setting the stage for max speed.

Lateral/2-plane swing (arms > 4" longer than height)—None. The setup procedure above should set you in a more erect posture, causing your shoulders to turn flatter and your arms to swing higher.

2-post/3-post with fast hips— Stand closer to the ball to better connect your arms to your body, keeping them in front of you when you turn. This also helps to center your contact.

For all rotary golfers, you know your posture is correct if your clubshaft and spine make a 90-degree angle.

The longer arms of a lateral (2-plane) golfer results in a more erect posture.

2. Stance Wdith

To find your perfect stance width, place two clubs on the ground, crossing them at a 90-degree angle [*photo, below*]. Set both feet inside the two clubs (alignment sticks also do the trick) and shuffle them inward until both your toes and heels contact with the shafts (measure the distance for future reference). This gets you in a good width for your short irons and wedges.

For 6-iron through hybrid, I recommend taking your natural stride and, after about three steps, pivot to your left on the heel of your right foot and the ball of your left foot. Your natural stride creates an ideal stance width for your longer clubs. Where your driver stance width is concerned, there's no method better than what you'll find on **gripsize.com**. Top 100 Teacher David Wright has develop what's arguably the most researched and calculated way to nail proper stance width for driver. Watch the video and never have to worry about this part of your setup again.

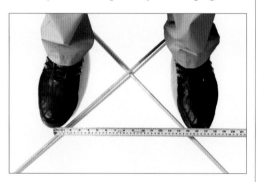

Use my stance drill to get a base width for your wedges, irons and hybrids, then visit **gripsize.com** to nail it for your driver.

ADJUSTMENTS: 2-PLANE GOLFER

If you tested out for a lateral (2-plane) swing in the Arm Length Test, you need to adjust your stance width to accommodate your extra-long arms. As a rule, widen your stance 1/2 " for every inch that your arms are longer than your height.

3. Foot Flare

Flaring one or both feet is a powerful way to control the pivot and speed in your motion, making sure everything is where it needs to be when you strike the ball. Here's how to dial it in perfectly.

If you're a slow-hips golfer, square both feet to the line. This reduces the distance your hips must travel on your downswing (effectively speeding them up) so they can sync up with your arms.

If you're a fast-hips golfer, flare out both feet to *increase* the distance they must travel on your downswing (effectively slowing them down) so your arms can sync up with your turn. Flaring the right foot also helps keep your heel down, which solves the typical problem of fast hips pulling the right heel off the turf too soon.

POST ADJUSTMENTS

2-Post/3-Post: Place your feet in between the shafts on the ground from the stance-width drill [*left*] while holding a club across the tops of your thighs. Turn your hips to the right. If your right leg begins to straighten, or you can't reach a point where the shaft across your thighs matches the one on the ground (45° to the target line), start flaring out your right foot and keep flaring until it frees up your turn to the point where you can get the shaft across your thighs to match the one on the ground [*photos, right*]. If you have to flare your right foot more than 45 degrees to do it, drop your right foot back to buy you more turn.

1-Post/2-Plane: Square your right foot and your flare your left. Getting the left-foot flare position is crucial. Using the bisecting shafts on the ground, take your stance and slightly flare out your left foot. Turn toward the target until your left leg straightens—ideally this should occur when the shaft across your thighs matches the one on the ground. If it locks up before, flare out your left foot, and keep flaring it until your left leg locks up at the same time the shaft across your thighs matches the one on the ground. If your left leg locks up early, your arms will whip past your body, causing a wrap hook. If it locks up late (after impact), you won't transfer max energy to the ball.

Right-foot flare is key for setting your right-side post correctly in a 2- or 3-post swing.

Left-foot flare is key in a 1-post or 2-plane swing to correctly time the straightening of your left leg.

4. Ball Position

When determining your ball position, there are certain things you must consider. First, realize that the bottom of the arc (low point) for every swing you make with any club is usually located opposite your left armpit. Second, since you want to contact the ball on the upswing when hitting your driver—after the low point of your arc—you need to tee the ball forward of this position. I recommend using the outside of your left shoulder as a guide, and then make the following ball-position adjustments based on your swing, post type and hip speed:

If you're a fast-hips golfer, move the ball back one slot (opposite your left armpit). Same goes if you're a 3-post player.

If you're a 2-post golfer, utilize the same ball position as the fast-hips or 3-post player above, especially if you have to drop your right foot back to buy yourself more turn on your backswing, placing you in position to attack the ball from inside the target line.

If you're a 2-plane golfer, play the ball forward one slot (a ball outside your left shoulder) to offset the fact that you start your downswing with a lateral shift toward the target.

GET IT RIGHT!
We tested over 100 golfers (PGA Tour players to 5-handicappers) and found that missing your ideal foot flare and ball position can result in a loss of up to 27 yards of distance, and up to 37 percent in accuracy.

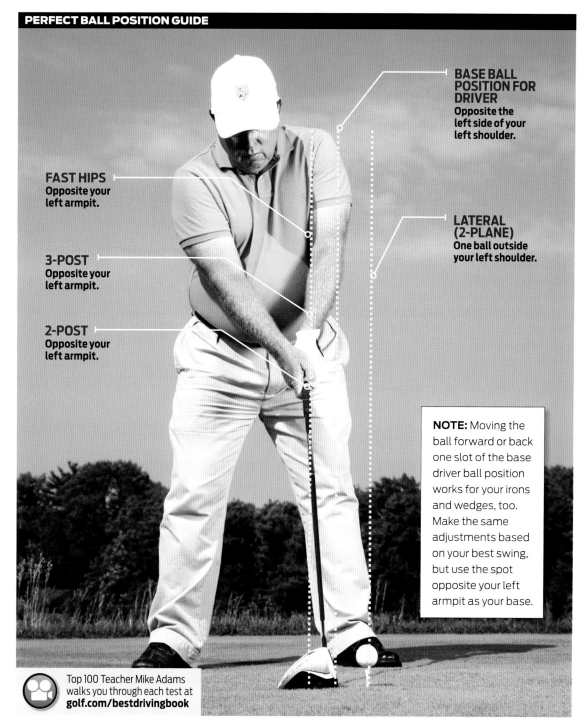

PERFECT BALL POSITION GUIDE

BASE BALL POSITION FOR DRIVER
Opposite the left side of your left shoulder.

FAST HIPS
Opposite your left armpit.

LATERAL (2-PLANE)
One ball outside your left shoulder.

3-POST
Opposite your left armpit.

2-POST
Opposite your left armpit.

NOTE: Moving the ball forward or back one slot of the base driver ball position works for your irons and wedges, too. Make the same adjustments based on your best swing, but use the spot opposite your left armpit as your base.

Top 100 Teacher Mike Adams walks you through each test at **golf.com/bestdrivingbook**

5. Grip

Your grip has multiple important functions, but the most critical job it has is to help you square the clubface at impact.

To find the one that's best for you, follow these guidelines:

If you have slow hips, use a weaker left-hand grip ("V" formed by thumb and forefinger pointing at the left side of your face). You can get away with a weaker hold since your hip turn isn't fast enough to whip the clubface open on your downswing.

If you have medium-speed hips, use a neutral left-hand grip ("V" pointing at your chin). You'll tend to get your hands a little ahead of the clubhead on your downswing with the face rotating open slightly, especially with longer clubs.

If you have fast hips, use a stronger left-hand grip ("V" pointing at your right shoulder). You need max control of the club to offset the fact that your hip speed causes the clubhead to lag behind your hands and open the clubface.

To really dial in the grip that best matches you and your swing, take your 5-iron and place the leading edge flush against a flat surface [*photos, right*]. Address the flat surface like it's the ball and get into your regular setup position. Next, turn your hips to the left in a mock-impact position while keeping your shoulders neutral, or square. If the clubface rotates open as you turn your hips, then it's evidence that you need a stronger left-hand hold (hand rotated to the right). Repeat the exercise after

strengthening your left hand, and keep on strengthening until the clubface remains square and flush to the surface after you turn your hips. Keep in mind that the stronger you make your grip, the more you'll have to forward-press your hands at address.

SLOW HIPS
Use a weaker left-hand hold ("V" pointing to the left side of your face).

MEDIUM-SPEED HIPS
Use a neutral left-hand hold ("V" pointing at your chin).

FAST HIPS
Use a stronger left-hand hold ("V" pointing to your right shoulder).

RIGHT-HAND ADJUSTMENTS

Your swing type also dictates how you set your right hand on the handle. Like all things with your grip, experimentation is key.
Lateral (2-plane) golfer: Set your right hand more on top of the grip (weaker, or rotated to the left).
Rotary (1-plane) golfer: Set your right hand more to the right (stronger, or rotated to the right).

HOW TO FINE-TUNE YOUR HOLD

START
Turn into a mock impact position after setting the face square to a flat surface.

NO!
If the face rotates open after you turn, your grip is too weak.

YES!
You nailed your grip strength if the face remains square after you turn.

BEST SET
Swing with your left arm only to find your natural hinge point.

6. Backswing

In order to track back like you want, perform the following drills to nail three key components of your backswing—length, wrist set and plane—and make your motion to the top smooth and effortless (these keys apply to every swing type).

DRILL: PERFECT WRIST SET

To find your natural "setting" position, grip any iron with your left hand only and swing it back using a smooth motion. As soon as your brain senses that the club has become heavy (it's constantly calculating what it needs to do to maintain control), it will motion you to set it in a lighter position by hinging your wrists. Use this same set position when you make real swings with both hands on the handle.

DRILL: PERFECT BACKSWING LENGTH

Kneel down while gripping any club. From this kneeling position, swing the club back while maintaining your posture [*photos, right*]. The length you can comfortably swing back is the one you should use on the course.

DRILL: PERFECT TRACK POSITION

To check if you're hitting your track correctly when you swing, have a friend set a shaft across your shoulders at address with the grip positioned where your right arm folds up to in the Elbow Hinge Test [*small photos, right*]. Swing to the top and stop (make sure your friend doesn't move the shaft). If you tracked correctly, then the shaft of your club should rest on the one your friend is holding [*big photos*]. If you're above or below the shaft, you're off plane. Repeat until you can hit your track every time.

Low-track golfer.

Mid-track golfer.

Your clubshaft sits perpendicular to your shoulders at address. Once you swing back and the shaft becomes parallel to the ground, your clubshaft should lie *parallel* to your shoulders [*photo, below*]. That, however, can change depending on your body type:

If you have a thin chest, your shoulders and shaft turn much later your backswing (your arms move first), so your clubshaft will be parallel to your toe line when it becomes parallel to the ground.

If you have a thick chest, your shoulders and shaft turn earlier (your thick chest stops your arms initially), so your clubshaft will be parallel to your shoulders, but inside the target line.

Regardless of your build, check that the shaft is perpendicular to your shoulders at the top. Even if you turn less than 90 degrees, your shaft should be perpendicular to your shoulders (look for the "T"). It might appear laid off, but that's only because you didn't rotate a full 90 degrees.

Ideal: Shaft parallel to shoulders when club parallel to the ground.

7. Release
There are three ways to deliver and release the club into the back of the ball: 1) with your hands and arms, 2) with your hips and, 3) with your trunk. Choose the one that best matches your best swing.

**2-POST/3-POST:
HIP RELEASE**
When you turn your upper body significantly more than your lower body during your backswing, you're basically creating the same separation you need at impact. Your goal, then, is to keep it intact. Start down by clearing your left hip, then feel like it's pulling your chest and shoulders through the impact zone. The key is to keep your left arm connected to your chest as you swing down and through impact.

**1-POST:
TRUNK RELEASE**
Just like the hip release, this one requires that you keep your arms connected to your chest going back and through. The difference is that it's powered by releasing your entire trunk (hips, chest and shoulders) and turning them together through impact, not pulling them into action with only your left hip.

**LATERAL (2-PLANE):
HAND-AND-ARM RELEASE**
Swing your hands and arms down and, as you approach the hitting zone, straighten your right arm while simultaneously folding your left elbow. This rotates the clubface from open to closed as it travels on its arc through the impact.

YOUR BEST SETUP & SWING ROAD MAP

I f you follow the tests and be honest with your results (don't cheat), you'll find your ideal setup and swing just by following the instructions in this chapter. Use the advice and information on the pages that follow to further refine your technique, and add power, speed and mobility for the longest drives of your golfing career. ●

Special thanks to instruction models Scott Chisholm, Paul Park and Renee Skidmore.

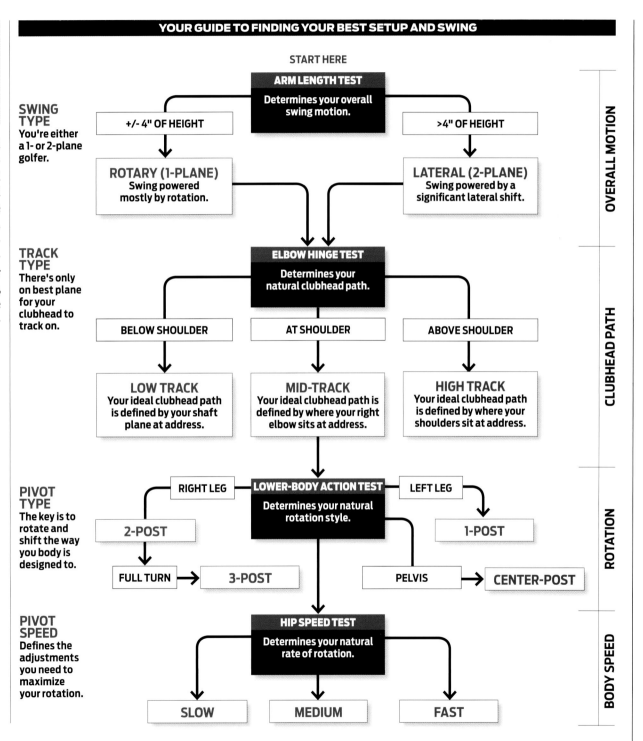

YOUR GUIDE TO FINDING YOUR BEST SETUP AND SWING

START HERE

ARM LENGTH TEST
Determines your overall swing motion.

+/- 4" OF HEIGHT

>4" OF HEIGHT

ROTARY (1-PLANE)
Swing powered mostly by rotation.

LATERAL (2-PLANE)
Swing powered by a significant lateral shift.

ELBOW HINGE TEST
Determines your natural clubhead path.

BELOW SHOULDER

AT SHOULDER

ABOVE SHOULDER

LOW TRACK
Your ideal clubhead path is defined by your shaft plane at address.

MID-TRACK
Your ideal clubhead path is defined by where your right elbow sits at address.

HIGH TRACK
Your ideal clubhead path is defined by where your shoulders sit at address.

RIGHT LEG

LOWER-BODY ACTION TEST
Determines your natural rotation style.

LEFT LEG

2-POST

1-POST

FULL TURN → 3-POST

PELVIS → CENTER-POST

HIP SPEED TEST
Determines your natural rate of rotation.

SLOW

MEDIUM

FAST

SWING TYPE
You're either a 1- or 2-plane golfer.

TRACK TYPE
There's only on best plane for your clubhead to track on.

PIVOT TYPE
The key is to rotate and shift the way you body is designed to.

PIVOT SPEED
Defines the adjustments you need to maximize your rotation.

OVERALL MOTION

CLUBHEAD PATH

ROTATION

BODY SPEED

1-POST/HIGH-MID SLOT DRIVER
TIGER WOODS

By ignoring biomechanics and his best swing, the former No. 1 is struggling

From 1999 to 2006, Tiger Woods was the undisputed world's best ball striker. He led the Tour in GIR every year and consistently hovered near the top in Total Driving. Since he began making well-publicized swing changes (starting in 2004), he has become shorter and noticeably more crooked while placing undue stress on his body (particularly his left knee). Tiger is a lesson in the damage you can do by ignoring biomechanics. He's a natural 3-post, mid-track, fast-hips golfer who's trying to swing like a 1-post, high-track fast-hips golfer. And it's not working out.

One thing that has remained constant is Woods' posture at address: it's still excellent, with his body in a balanced, athletic position and the shaft pointing 90 degrees to his spine. He powers the club back nicely with the triangle created between his arms and shoulders, but then attempts to rotate around his left leg, causing his shoulders to steepen [*Frame 3*] and the club to prematurely rise to his shoulder plane (when Tiger hit it best his club traveled back and down on his right-arm plane).

The speed is there, but his new, aggressive slotting action [*Frame 9*] is making the ball go everywhere. And even though he's approaching from the inside, the clubhead moves left after impact much earlier than when he drove it longer and straighter than anybody else.

1

2

Triangle created between his shoulders and arms motion the club back. Perfect.

6

7

11

When he drove it best, Tiger swung more out to the right.

12

3

KEY MISTAKE

His new 1-post turn forces the club to track above his natural plane.

4

5

8

9

KEY MISTAKE

Big-time slotting action is taking its toll on his body and stats.

10

13

14

15

CHAPTER 4

You laid the groundwork for your best swing in Chapter 3. Here's how to refine it and truly make it your own.

HOW TO *UNLOCK* YOUR DRIVER SWING CODE

Building on your basic swing model type by applying key in-swing moves and positions gives you efficiency, consistency and a driver swing you'll love for life

By **E.A. TISCHLER, PGA**
*New Horizons Golf
Approach, San Jose, Calif.*

THE NOTION OF A "PERFECT SWING" is a well-debated one in teaching circles. Some instructors believe that a perfect swing exists which all golfers are free to employ. Others argue that there's a standard model which addresses many key fundamentals, yet at the same time believe there are different ways to apply these fundamentals based on body-type characteristics. Then there are the instructors who believe in a variety of acceptable models, and that the variety exists either because differences in body types dictate the need, or that it makes sense to provide a wealth options from which the student can choose.

I subscribe to the theory that there's definitely a "best swing" for every golfer, and believe in the existence of a carefully calculated process for identifying and developing it. If you performed the tests in the previous chapter, then you're already well on your way to finding this best swing. The next step is to refine the results of the Chapter 3 tests so that you can accurately pinpoint the fundamentals, biomechanical features and techniques you'll need to get down to the business of owning your swing.

The trick is to stick with your method once you learn what it is. Consistency is the key. If you're constantly—or even periodically—changing techniques, then you'll never reach your true driving and scoring potential. Unfortunately, it takes much longer to internalize your skills than it does to understand them. This is why you've abandoned techniques in the past—you quit and search for another method before you internalize the one you're playing with. When you determine what your best swing is by following the instructions in this book, don't make this mistake.

On the following pages, I (along with instruction legends Jim Hardy and Jim McLean) will explain the biomechanical features (options, really) that you'll need in order to take what you learned in the previous chapter and truly make your best swing your own. Because of space limitations, I can't cover every feature. Instead, I'll touch on those that are most relevant to the collaborated efforts of this book.

There are 12 biomechanical features I use to help golfers understand their structure [*below*]. The ones I'll discuss in this chapter to help you define your best swing are in red:

1.	Swing path	**7.**	Clearing action
2.	Swing track	**8.**	Axis of symmetry
3.	Wrist lever action	**9.**	Swing linkage
4.	Lever delivery action	**10.**	Swing slotting
5.	Swing anchor	**11.**	Postural release
6.	Torque system	**12.**	Arc management

It's interesting to note that four of these features relate to accuracy (Nos. 1-4), four have to do with power (Nos. 5-8) and four relate to feel (Nos. 9-12). Thus, in building your best swing you're creating one that's accurate, powerful and that provides a feeling which allows you to repeat it without working to achieve uncomfortable positions and angles. In other words, your best swing is easy to make.

PART 1:
REFINING YOUR BEST SWING

Once you're able to accept the fact that your body structure determines the type of actions that are available to you (which you should following Mike Adams' convincing arguments in the previous chapter), then you need to assess your body type—and by that I mean your physiological as well as your athletic attributes [*see Chapters 5 and 8 for more detail*]. These considerations will guide you in the direction of the techniques that are best suited for your needs. When you take these body-type assessments keep in mind that though you might not always like the results, it's important to adhere to them. If you choose not to, not only will your golf shots likely be bad, but you run a very serious risk of injury. The reason for this is that the guidance provided is based on sound biomechanical theory, which simply cannot be ignored.

Yes, when it comes to the biomechanics of your swing your options are few and far between. In fact, experience tells me that these are pretty much set in stone. The biomechanical makeup of your swing is what it is because of the way your body is structured, and it's nearly impossible to change how your body is put together. For example, studies show that golfers who undergo hip-replacement surgery usually apply the same biomechanical feature/options they used before the operation. If you fight your body mechanics and your structure, then you'll struggle—and eventually fail. Even the most talented and athletic professionals on Tour experience difficulty when they try to fight their inherent biomechanics. Yet, the fight con-

There are swing style choices and then there are absolutes—fundamentals dictated by your inherent biomechanics that can't be ignored.

"If you fight your body mechanics and your structure, then you'll struggle—and eventually fail."

tinues, because it's perfectly plausible for you to play decent golf without adhering to the options your body dictates. However, doing so usually ends up in injury because bad applications will constantly be working against your framework. Instead, don't fight your physical abilities and limitations, embrace them. You'll start swinging better as a result.

STEP 1: Refine Your Track

GOAL: *Know where you need to be at the top.*

As Mike Adams demonstrated in Chapter 3, there are three track options: low, medium and high. He discusses these primarily as backswing clubhead paths (and potential delivery paths—more on that later in this chapter). My system is based on how your body is arranged at the *top* of your backswing ("top of your track"), yet applies the same nomenclature. It's important to define your top of the track because it takes into account the movement in your elbows and forearms as you elevate the club in your backswing, and because it sets the stage for any slotting moves you make in your delivery. Some of you will find you have the greatest lever-age in a low-track alignment at the top. Others are engineered to get into a mid-track alignment and the rest in a high-track alignment. In order for you to discover where you need to be at the top of your backswing, you must investigate how you arms and elbows function most efficiently within the tracking corridor you tested for on page 37. For now, simply be aware that your top position is dictated by your structure just like every other segment of your swing.

THE TRACK-ELBOW DYNAMIC

LOW TRACK
Left arm below your right shoulder.

MID-TRACK
Left arm through your right shoulder.

HIGH TRACK
Left arm above your right shoulder.

Before fold...

...after fold.

Before fold...

...after fold.

Before fold...

...after fold.

If you test out as a low-track golfer, your elbows should move more around your torso—or horizontal to the ground—before you fold your right arm to elevate the club. When you do fold your right elbow, your club will track to a low position.

If you test out as a mid-track golfer, your left elbow should raise during your takeaway while your right elbow stays down. This cambering action sets the club in the mid-track position (left arm through shoulder) once you fold your right arm.

If you test out as a high-track golfer, you should lift both elbows as you start your backswing. This lifting action results in a higher top of the track once your fold you right elbow and elevate the club in your backswing.

STEP 2: Refining Your Swing Path

GOAL: *Discover your ideal arm and elbow action.*

The movement of your right forearm throughout your swing is important to defining your best swing. Basically, the manner in which it functions dictates your top-of-the-track position and—to a certain extent—your delivery position. As you read on the previous page, track and right-arm action go hand-in-hand. This is the reason why I developed a test to determine how your right arm is deigned to operate. Armed with the knowledge of your right-arm biomechanics, you can nail your path (using the Elbow Hinge Test in Chapter 3 as your base) and your top of the track. My test focuses on the alignment of your right forearm. It can face the sky (under alignment), the target (side-on alignment) or the ground (on-top alignment).

TAKE THE TEST: To determine your best method for swinging the club back to the top, grab a medicine ball (a volleyball also works) and assume your golf posture.

 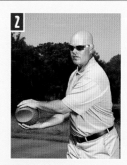 

1. UNDER-ALIGNMENT TEST
Set your right hand under the ball and your left hand directly on top with your elbows slightly in front of your rib cage. Turn to your right and then fold your right elbow to get to a mock top position. Have a friend apply downward pressure to the ball. Note how strongly you're able to resist.

2. SIDE-ON ALIGNMENT TEST
Set your hands on both sides of the ball with your elbows slightly ahead of your rib cage. Next, pull your right elbow back to where it's even with the side seam on your shirt. Then, turn to your right and fold your right elbow to get to a mock top position. Have a friend apply downward pressure to the ball. Note how strongly you're able to resist.

3. ON-TOP ALIGNMENT TEST
Set your right hand on top of the ball and your left hand directly below with your elbows slightly in front of your rib cage. Next, pull your right elbow back behind the side seam on your shirt. Then, turn to your right and fold your right elbow to get to a mock top position. Have a friend apply downward pressure to the ball. Note how strongly you're able to resist.

TEST KEY:
The alignment that best allows you to resist downward pressure is your best backswing motion.

There's an associated path for every type of forearm alignment [*photos, right*]. You can also think of your right forearm alignments in terms of performing dumbbell curls in the gym. The standard curl uses an under alignment, the hammer curl uses a side-on alignment, and the reverse curl an on-top alignment. I actually recommend that you perform the appropriate curl in the gym once you know how your body is structured.

UNDER SWING PATH

Right forearm faces up.

Right elbow in front of shirt seam.

If you tested out for under alignment, your best path is the **Under Swing Path**. Think of sliding your hands under a small box to pick it up and carry it. As the box rests in the palms of your hands, your forearms face upward. Under golfers tend to position the right elbow in front of the body and above the right hip bone to help facilitate structural leverage.

SIDE-ON SWING PATH

Right forearm faces target.

Right elbow even with shirt seam.

If you tested out for side-on alignment, your best path is the **Side-On Swing Path**. Think of using the handles on the sides of a box to pick it up. As you take hold of the handles and lift the box your forearms face inward (or side-on as I call it). Side-on golfers tend to marry their right arm to the right side of their body when they swing.

ON-TOP SWING PATH

Right forearm faces ground.

Right elbow behind shirt seam.

If you tested out for on-top alignment, your best path is the **On-Top Swing Path**. Think of what you would do to get up on a counter top. You'd position your hands—palms down—on the counter and begin to push down on it to help lift your body upward. In this case, your forearms face downward. Over-swing path golfers tend to pull their elbows back behind the seamline of their shirt and pinch their shoulder blades together.

STEP 3: Using Path to Nail Your Track

GOAL: *Discover your ideal arm and elbow action.*

Combining your results in the Swing Path test on the previous page with the base knowledge of your ideal backswing clubhead path (Elbow Hinge Test, page 37) allows you to nail your top-of-the-track position (i.e., where you want to be at the end of your backswing). For some, tracking back and forth on the ideal plane based on the results of the Elbow Hinge Test works. If, however, you tested out in a gray area, or wish to validate the results of the test, follow the steps at right.

TAKE THE TEST
Using a medicine ball (a volleyball or similar-sized object works just as well), assume your best alignment setup based on the results of the previous test (I'm an under-alignment golfer, so I'll demonstrate from this position with my right hand on the underside of the ball). Then turn to the right using the appropriate elbow and forearm action based on your alignment.

Swing back to the low-track top position, with your left arm below your right shoulder. Have a friend apply downward pressure to the ball. Note how strongly you're able to resist.

Return to your start position, then swing back to the mid-track top position, with your left arm bisecting your right shoulder. Have a friend apply downward pressure to the ball. Note how strongly you're able to resist.

This time, swing back to the high-track top position. Note how strongly you're able to resist when your friend applies the downward pressure.

TEST KEY: The track position that allows you to resist the most is your best top of backswing position.

STEP 4: Refining Your Best Wrist Action

GOAL: *Find your ideal hinge.*

This is the feature that governs your wrist hinge alignments. There are three options: vertical, horizontal and diagonal. As was the case for the swing track and swing path features on the previous pages, wrist lever action can be tested for its structural soundness. Take the test to find the one that best fits your biomechanical structure.

TAKE THE TEST
Get into your address position, then hinge the club up so that the shaft is parallel to the ground.

VERTICAL HINGE

Without moving out of your address posture, hinge the club straight up toward your nose and hold (vertical hinge action). Have a friend apply pressure to the shaft in the direction of your eyes. Note how strongly you resist.

Return to the start position, and this time hinge your wrists so that the shaft moves diagonally toward your right shoulder (diagonal hinge action). Have a friend apply pressure to the shaft in the direction of your right shoulder. Note how strongly you resist.

DIAGONAL HINGE

HORIZONTAL HINGE

Return to the start position, and hinge your wrists so that the shaft moves parallel to the ground. Stop cocking when the clubhead is in line with your hands. Have a friend apply pressure to the shaft in the direction of your body. Note how strongly you resist.

Biomechanically, your wrist lever action determines the alignment of the clubface at the top of the backswing [*consult Chapter 5*]. Although you can manipulate it, executing your backswing with the swing track, swing path and wrist lever action that match your body mechanics sets the clubface square to your arc. Keep in mind that each of the three wrist lever actions are valid and effective—if you own them. As with the other options, 33 percent of golfers are built to own the vertical option, 33 percent are built to own the diagonal option, and 33 percent of golfers are built to own the horizontal option.

> **TEST KEY:**
> **The hinge that allows you to resist the most is your best lever action.**

STEP 5: Refining Your Lever Delivery

The first three features I've described establish your best arm-swing alignments so that you can efficiently and precisely employ structural leverage within your swing. In order to deliver the levered energy you need an action. I call this action the "release." However, it's more precise to call it the "Lever Delivery Action." It, too has three options: covering, cornering and extending.

IF YOU TESTED OUT FOR UNDER-ALIGNMENT...

USE THE EXTENDING DELIVERY ACTION

As soon as your left arm gets parallel to the ground in your downswing, straighten it—but do so while maintaining the angle in your wrists. As your right arm extends you should feel like your right palm is facing the ground. The feeling you're after is to "cover the ball" at impact.

Since the covering delivery action happens in a downward action, you need to respond by launching upward to make room for the extension. This will help accelerate your clubhead while at the same time providing a precise delivery. The by-product is effortless swing power with maximum precision and efficiency.

Once the club gets parallel to the ground in your downswing...

...straighten your right arm.

IF YOU TESTED OUT FOR SIDE-ON ALIGNMENT...

USE THE CORNERING LEVER DELIVERY ACTION

As soon as the butt end of the club points at the ball in your downswing (with your left arm approximately 45 degrees to the ground), straighten your right arm. Try to extend it to a point approximately 45 degrees past the ball. As your right arm finishes straightening, unhinge your wrists. It should feel like the clubhead is "turning the corner" along with your swing arc.

It's important to note that as you reach the end of your cornering delivery, you must counter-balance its force (and facilitate acceleration) by posting up with your left leg as soon as the delivery action begins. Then, as your wrists unhinge, move your head and sternum up and back away from the extension point.

Once the butt of the club points at the ball...

...extend your right arm to 45 degrees past the impact point.

IF YOU TESTED OUT FOR ON-TOP ALIGNMENT...

USE THE COVERING LEVER DELIVERY ACTION

As soon as your left arm gets parallel to the ground in your downswing, straighten it—but do so while maintaining the angle in your wrists. As your right arm extends you should feel like your right palm is facing the ground. The feeling you're after is to "cover the ball" at impact.

Since the covering delivery action happens in a downward action, you need to respond by launching upward to make room for the extension. This will help accelerate your clubhead while at the same time providing a precise delivery. The by-product is effortless swing power with maximum precision and efficiency.

Once your left arm gets parrallel to the ground...

...extend your right arm out toward the target.

"An important point to realize is that for each of the delivery options, extending your right arm begins at a different point in your downswing. Also, the aim point is different as is the completion point. However, the time between delivery to extension is the same for all three options."

STEP 6: Refining Your Swing Anchor

GOAL: *Discover the best way to anchor your weight and rotate back and through.*

A nother key biomechanical feature is what I call your swing anchor. This feature involves your body's best pivot point [*see Chapter 3*] in coordination with a counter-balance point. It's organized to centralize your pivot action, which helps minimize or even eliminate any drifting or swaying in your swing.

What determines your body's best pivot point is how your body is balanced. Some golfers are built to pivot more efficiently around the left hip joint (1-post), around the rear hip joint (2- and 3-post) and around the centerline of the body (center post). Keep in mind that you may have more bone and/or muscle mass on one side of the body than the other, or a spinal or postural condition that will encourage your body to be balanced more to one side or the other.

TAKE THE TEST
Utilizing Mike Adams' Lower-Body Action Test [*page 42*] helps you determine which swing anchor fits you best. I suggest you validate the results by hitting a few quarter-speed shots with your feet close together and with 1) your right foot back, 2) both feet even and, 3) your left foot back.

FRONT ANCHOR
If you're able to maintain your balance and make solid contact with your right foot pulled back, then you're a front-anchor golfer (1-post). Your body prefers to rotate around your front hip.

REAR ANCHOR
If you're able to maintain your balance and make solid contact with your left foot pulled back, then you're a rear-anchor golfer (2- or 3-post). Your body prefers to rotate around your rear hip.

CENTER ANCHOR
If you're able to maintain your balance and make solid contact with your feet together, then you're a center-anchor golfer. Your body prefers to rotate around your pelvis, or centerline.

TEST KEY:
The stance from which you make the best contact tells you where you should anchor your weight and what you should rotate around during your swing.

Making the Most of Your Anchor

One of the keys to maintaining a sound swing anchor is to establish it at address, and then maintaining a stationary head until you have reached your full extension (or at least keep it as stationary as possible with the appropriate counter actions in play). What that means is that a front-anchor golfer's head should be ahead of center of the stance, a rear-anchor golfer's head should be behind the center of the stance, and a center-anchor golfer's head should be in line with the center of the stance. Keep in mind these are general recommendations since the secondary tilt alignments needed for good posturing through the ball may move their locations slightly.

FRONT ANCHOR

1. Step in with your left foot first.
2. Take your stance and set your weight over your left leg.
3. Rotate over your left leg going back.
4. Rotate over your left leg coming down.

CENTER ANCHOR

1. Stand with both feet together.
2. Take your stance and set your weight evenly over both legs.
3. Rotate over your center going back.
4. Rotate over your center coming down.

REAR ANCHOR

1. Step in with your right foot first.
2. Take your stance and set your weight over your right leg.
3. Rotate over your right leg going back.
4. Rotate over your right leg coming down.

STEP 7: Refining Your Best Torque

GOAL: *Discover the ideal way to load up on your backswing.*

Traditionally, torque is described as coiling the upper body on top of a resisted lower body. This is a conventional view, since torque can also be created in the transition, and it can be produced in the lower body as well as throughout the entire body. As with all other features there are three ways to create torque: lower, upper and full.

TAKE THE TEST
To discover the best way for you to turn and load up on your backswing, sit on a chair with your back straight and your feet about hip-width apart. Place a club across your shoulders as shown and then turn your shoulders to the right as far as you comfortably can without moving your head.

IF YOU CAN'T TURN MORE THAN 45 DEGREES, YOU'RE A LOWER-TORQUE GOLFER

Lower torque is produced by establishing a grounded stance, and then turning your hips generously in the backswing. The upper body also turns freely, and there may be a slight amount of torque transferred to the torso. However, the majority of torque is produced throughout the legs. This option is mainly used by golfers with short torsos and restrictions in their ability to achieve a significant differential between their hips and shoulder turns.

Because of your very limited range of motion, load up by turning your lower body and hug the ground with your feet.

IF YOU CAN TURN

The full torque option is the view of playing power golf from the ground up. You establish it by either rotating your shoulders first (which pulls your hips into action, followed by your knees and then your grounded feet), or you can lead with your hips. Either way, a full-torque player is best suited to turn everything.

GREES (NOT MUCH MORE), YOU'RE A FULL-TORQUE GOLFER

IF YOU CAN TURN A SOLID 90 DEGREES, YOU'RE AN UPPER-TORQUE GOLFER

The flexibility inherent in a upper-torque golfer allows him or her to create torque using the traditionally taught method: turning the shoulders to the max while resisting with a stable lower body (i.e., more shoulder turn than hip turn).

Because of your limited range of motion, load up by turning your upper body and lower body in equal amounts.

Because of your extended range of motion, load up by turning your upper body while resisting with your hips.

STEP 8: Refining Your Best Slot

The last biomechanical feature we will discuss is the swing slotting feature. Its three options include hip-plane slotting, torso-plane slotting and shoulder plane slotting. The basic image of slotting is the plane the club is delivered along through impact. You might also say that your swing slotting action is the dynamic that governs your downswing plane, whereas your swing track action governs your backswing plane.

HIP-PLANE SLOT (SHAFT PLANE)

The hip-plane slotting option uses what I call a down-slotting action to position the clubshaft at an angle that's aligned through the hip girdle and directed toward the target line. It's the plane the shaft generally sits on at address, and is often described as the address plane. In general, golfers that talk about returning the clubshaft through impact at the same plane angle it was aligned at address are advocating a hip-plane slot method.

TORSO-PLANE SLOT (RIGHT ARM PLANE)

The torso-plane slot option uses what I call a cross-slotting action to position the clubshaft so that it can be delivered at an angle that's aligned through the torso and directed toward the target line. I call it cross-slotting because golfers that perform it describe the feel of the action as moving across the chest and down toward the ball. They also describe the feeling of the left arm crossing over the chest in the backswing and the right arm across the chest in the through-swing.

SHOULDER-PLANE SLOT (SHOULDER PLANE)

The shoulder-plane slot uses what I call a cutting-the-plane action to position the clubshaft so that it can be delivered at an angle that's aligned through the shoulder girdle and directed toward the target line. This option has the most direct slotting pattern from transition through the ball. By that I mean it takes little or zero shifting to be positioned in the slot. And since it's performed without a significant shift, it is often described as having a cutting-the-plane feel.

Take the Test: Finding Your Best Slot

GOAL: *Discover the ideal way to deliver the clubhead.*

1

Get into your normal address position with a driver.

2

Hinge and rotate your wrists to set the club while keeping your hands in their address position (under your chest). Have a friend apply upward pressure to the shaft in the direction of your left arm. Note how strongly you're able to resist.

3

Return to your address position. This time, hinge and rotate your wrists to set the club while raising your arms so that your hands are directly below your nose. Have a friend apply upward pressure to the shaft in the direction of your left arm. Note how strongly you're able to resist.

4

Return to your address position, then hinge and rotate your wrists to set the club while raising your arms so that your hands are outside the tip of your forehead. Have a friend apply upward pressure to the shaft in the direction of your left arm. Note how strongly you're able to resist.

If you resisted best with your hands under your chest, your preferred delivery position is **the hip slot.**

If you resisted best with your hands under your nose, your preferred delivery position is **the torso slot.**

If you resisted best with your hands outside the tip of your forehead, your preferred delivery position is **the shoulder slot.**

TEST KEY:
The hand position that allows you to resist the most is your best slot.

Slotting Guide

HIP SLOT

Deliver the club to the ball on the plane defined by the clubshaft at address using predominantly hip power.

LOW TRACK

Top-of-track position defined by left arm below right shoulder.

MID TRACK

Top-of-track position defined by left arm bisecting right shoulder.

HIGH TRACK

Top-of-track position defined by left arm above right shoulder.

TORSO SLOT

Deliver the club to the ball on the plane defined by your right arm at address using predominantly torso power.

SHOULDER SLOT

Deliver the club to the ball on the plane defined by your shoulders at address using predominantly shoulder power.

All the fundamental principles, biomechanical feature/options and techniques discussed in this chapter have been employed successfully, efficiently and precisely by great players. And that's the case because bodies truly are structured differently from golfer to golfer. Thus, great golfers simply find a way to utilize their unique body characteristics to execute a fundamentally as well as a biomechanically sound swing.

By studying the principles in this book, in combination with both inner- and mental-game techniques, you can develop a swing that fits you perfectly—a swing that can be owned for a lifetime. Keep in mind, the definitive tests are designed to show you how your body is structured so that you can understand the biomechanical influences in your swings.

This book can certainly help you understand what your best options are and by understanding them you will be well on your way to owning your swing. The next step is putting it into action using the timing, tempo and feel you need to make your new best swing natural for you on the course. For this purpose **I've developed five special drills you can use to make your swing your own and groove it's specific parts so you can repeat it over and over.** Visit golf.com/bestdrivingbook and I'll walk you through this practice regimen and show how each drill pulls all of the different parts of your swing—track, anchor, turn, torque, slot and delivery—together.

"All the principles, biomechanical feature/options and techniques discussed in this chapter have been employed successfully, efficiently and precisely by great players."

Watch E.A. Tischler perform his "best swing" practice drills at **golf.com/bestdrivingbook.**

PART 2:
THE TRUTH ABOUT 1- AND 2-PLANE SWINGS

GOLF MAGAZINE TOP 100 TEACHERS IN AMERICA

By **JIM HARDY, PGA**
Plane Truth Golf
Spring, Tex.
2007 PGA Teacher of the Year

For more in-depth information on the one- and two-plane swings, and how to incorporate them into your game, check out **The Plane Truth for Golfers Master Class** by Jim Hardy with John Andrisani, or visit www.planetruthgolf.com.

I view all golf swings as having two motors—the body and the arms/club. I believe both motors must be running to produce an effective swing. The body motor's primary responsibility is to supply the pivot or turning motion, while the arm/club motor's job is to swing and deliver the clubface to the ball. In relation to the body, the arm/club motor will always swing in one of two ways: on somewhat the same plane as the body is pivoting or on a distinctly different plane. I call these two variations the one-plane swing (body and arms on the same plane), and the two-plane swing (body and arms move on distinctly different planes).

To visualize the two swing types, imagine the 1-plane swing like a baseball hitter's motion, only bent over so it is oriented towards the ground. Examples of one-plane swingers are Ben Hogan, Ricky Fowler, Anthony Kim, Rory McElroy, and Hunter Mahan. The 2-plane swing is one in which the arms swing more vertically while the body turns. Examples of two plane swingers are Jack Nicklaus, Tom Watson, Bubba Watson, David Toms, Nick Watney, and Colin Montgomery, among others.

The two swing types are significantly different and it's up to you to determine if you are a 1-plane or 2-plane swinger. A good test is to ask yourself honestly if you feel better when bending over at address and swinging your arms and club around your chest while you pivot or if you prefer standing fairly erect at address and keeping your arms and club in front of your chest, swinging them more up and down while you

Finding the right type of swing for your game is critical for hitting your best shots.

pivot. Another good test is hitting balls off side hill lies. If the ball above your feet is easier to hit than the ball below your feet then you are probably a 1-plane swinger. If swinging more up and down to hit the ball below your feet is easier then you are probably a 2-planer. Regardless of

what you think now, read the advice for both swing types with an open mind and I'm sure one swing method will appeal to you more than the other. Once you do find the swing type that fits your natural tendencies you'll be well on your way to greater consistency and better scores.

2-Plane Power Driving

Because the 2-plane swing features a high and somewhat vertical arm and club position at the top of the backswing, a downward, powerful leverage motion is built into the swing. What isn't built into a 2-plane swing is a shallow angle of approach. That must be a result of the body motor and the arm motor working in tandem during the downswing. One hallmark of the 2-plane swing that is different from the one-plane swing is the need for timing, tempo and rhythm. One-plane swings can be pretty fast because the two motors are on somewhat the same plane. Two-plane swings have the two motors running in distinctly different planes. Because of this the two motors must be timed together. If you get out of timing or tempo or rhythm you can easily lose your ability to strike the ball solidly. As a result, the power for the 2-plane swing is leverage and force, not just speed.

SETUP

At address your body should be fairly upright, which puts the hips and shoulders closer to the same plane. This is critical because a two-plane swing requires maximum hip rotation in order to function properly. In fact, the greatest two-plane swinger of all time, Jack Nicklaus, said he always tried to turn his hips as fully as possible in order to create the power he wanted. If you decide to go with a 2-plane swing you'll need to do the same or your downswing will get overly steep, which will produce nothing but glancing blows and slices. To hit solid drives you need a shallow angle of attack.

STAND TALL
Two-plane swingers need to stand more upright—this swing will produce leverage.

HIPS ARE KEY
You'll need to rotate as much as possible if you want to create the desired speed.

TILT 'EM
Your right shoulder must sit lower than left.

PLAY IT UP
Make sure you tee the ball forward in your stance.

BACKSWING

While the hips are turning as much as possible the arms need to swing inward and upward into a position above the right shoulder. The club should be pointed either at the target or slightly across the line to the right of the target. It's also OK to allow your head to move a bit behind the ball as you transfer weight into your right leg.

Don't try to lock your head in place. Instead, let it move.

Your hands need to be nice and high at the top.

Get ready to drop your hands aggressively from the top.

Then start your downswing with a sliding left hip.

DOWNSWING

For a powerful downswing both motors (arms and body) have to be engaged at the start of the downswing. The body's initial move from the top should be a lateral slide of the left hip without any shoulder turn. This slide then needs to be combined with a powerful downward chopping motion of the arms and club. Some call this move, "dropping it into the slot," though I prefer to think of it as a smooth yet aggressive drop of the arms and club.

THE 2-PLANE SWING: AROUND AND UP LEADS TO LEVERAGE

A fairly erect posture is key for 2-planers.

The head should move behind the ball here.

The club moves inward as it moves upward.

Two-planers get the hands nice and high at the top.

A lateral slide of the left hip keys the downsing.

IMPACT

Immediately after the initiation of the downswing, the right hip should start turning with some thrust towards the ball. This is critical for shallowing out the plane of the arms and club as they approach impact, which is necessary for solid driving. By incorporating a slight thrust into the turning of the right hip, the arms will fall in behind the right hip and the clubface will open a bit. This position slightly behind the right hip guarantees a shallow hit while the opening clubface gives you an additional source of power; a hard closing release with the wrists and forearms of the clubface during impact. This is where the 2-planer shines—applying plenty of leverage to the ball.

The left hip leads followed by the hands and club.

Keep turning all the way until the ball is long gone.

FOLLOW-THROUGH

Your body should continue turning through impact, staying in pace with the arm swing. The primary power source in the 2-plane swing is the leverage and force of the arm/club motor, but two other factors add to it and create additional power. One is the closing release of the wrists and forearms, and the other is the body, which, heading into impact, is set up with the lower body forward and the upper body slightly trailing. This adds to the speed and upward hit as it turns through impact.

The club is beginning to move from out to in.

Arms deliver plenty of leverage into impact.

The release of the wrists and forearms adds more power.

Upper body has caught up to the lower by now.

High hands in the finish mirror the backswing.

DRILL 1: Fix Your Reverse Pivot

Hold a club across the front of your shoulders and assume your address posture for the 2-plane swing. Turn your shoulders fully, on an angle that is bent forward 10 to 20 degrees from horizontal. Check that the clubshaft (which represents the turning angle of your shoulders) is pointing to the right of the ball and beyond, or outside of, the zone that runs from the ball to a spot on the ground 48 inches beyond it. Return to address and repeat several times.

DRILL 2: Widen Your Backswing Arc

Set up as you normally would for a 2-plane swing. Then practice making a start to the backswing in which you turn your shoulders and hips, along with the club, to a position where the clubshaft is parallel to the ground halfway back.

When the club reaches this position, your torso should also have turned nearly 90-degrees, which is to say it is nearly facing the same way as the clubshaft is pointing. Pause for a moment, then complete the backswing (as well as the drill) from there by simply folding your arms and the club up to the top. Repeat several times. This drill teaches you to increase the speed of the turning of your body in relation to the lifting of the club with your arms.

DRILL 3: Delay Your Shoulder Turn

Swing your driver to the top of the backswing position. Hold the position for a second, then with your shoulders turned, slide your left or lead hip laterally toward your target. This lateral hip slide should be strong enough that your knees are also pulled laterally and your weight moves onto your left foot. As you make this lateral hip slide, let your arms, hands, and the club, drop straight down. Your wrists should be cocked so that the club shaft is still angled upward.

1-Plane Power Driving

Because the 1-plane swing is more rotational and somewhat flatter than the 2-plane swing, the shallow angle of approach needed to swing up slightly at the ball is inherent in the motion. What isn't built into the swing is leverage. If you're a one-plane swinger you need to find a power source other than leverage. That source is rotational power that produces the centrifugal effect of speed in a circle. To do this your arm and club motor must engage with the body at the start of the downswing to immediately create an outward force in the clubhead and an inward force in the arms and clubshaft.

ADDRESS

At address your body must be bent over enough that a club lying perpendicular to the shoulders and also perpendicular to the spine angle would point to a spot around 2 to 3 feet beyond the ball. If the shaft points beyond 4 feet, you need to bend over more.

BACKSWING

You need to turn your hips and shoulders back as far as possible while still maintaining the spine angle you established at address. You'll notice that you will naturally build up a great deal of torque between your hips and shoulders, and that's what you want. While turning your body, your left arm should move across your chest in three particular ways; it stays tight to the left side of your chest, it stays low on the chest, and it extends as far across the chest as possible. The right arm and in particular the right elbow, has to move upward and backward as well as away from the body in the first half of the backswing.

Hands and arms swing around the body, not up.

Pull the handle downward and inward for increased speed.

DOWNSWING

First, your left leg and left hip must pull backward and slightly towards the target while at the same time your right shoulder turns outward and downward. It's this combination that gets the correct rotational motion started. You absolutely cannot reverse the motion and start with the right hip turning outward—if you do you will completely come up out of your posture. Next, your arms should sling the clubhead out toward the ball while pulling the handle of the club downward and inward as close to your right hip as possible.

THE 1-PLANE SWING: ROTATE WITH SPEED FOR MAX POWER

One-planers must bend over more at address.

Arms and club stay close to the body in the takeaway.

A restricted hip turn builds torque as the body rotates.

Left arm must move across the chest, not up in the air.

Body and arms must rotate together on the way down.

Arms and handle move in through impact.

IMPACT

The key now is to create even more speed through the ball. You should accomplish this with the same motion a figure skater employs to spin ever faster and faster, by pulling your arms in close to your body. It is this "tight arms to the body," effort that accomplishes two power related things. It allows the inward centripetal pull to create even greater outward centrifugal force and also allows the body to turn even faster. Just like that figure skater, the tighter the arms the faster the body rotates.

Club is thrown to the left by the powerful rotation.

FOLLOW-THROUGH

Both motors are now engaged in an ultimate effort to supply rotational power into the ball. To finish it off, allow the body to throw the arms around to the left and into the finish. The arms go off the body and upward only after they have been thrown around, low and to the left.

Move the clubhead out and the handle down and in.

Arms and club move into the body for increased speed.

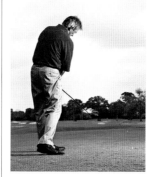

Body must continue to turn quickly past impact.

Rotation of the body throws the club out to the left.

Arms go off the body and up only in the finish.

1-PLANE DRILLS

DRILL 1: Object In the Sky

Stand in the 1-plane address position and imagine that an object such as an airplane is in the air directly behind and above you. Execute your backswing turn, making certain that you turn your entire chest to the right. At the top of the backswing, turn your head to the right. You should be in a position where you can see the object out of the corner of your right eye. From the top of the backswing, turn 180 degrees through impact, keeping your turn in the zone all the way to the finish. Your shoulders and hips should be facing the target, and you should still have some forward bend toward the zone in your spine. Turn your head to the left. You should be able to see the object with your left eye.

DRILL 2: Glove Under Arm

Place a golf glove (or head cover) underneath your left arm so your upper left arm holds it against your chest. Take a three-quarter-length backswing while keeping the glove secured between your upper left arm and chest. Make a series of these three-quarter backswings and see if you can continue to hold the glove in place. After you have gained command of the backswing motion, do the drill completely by making a three-quarter backswing, then a three-quarter downswing, while keeping the glove trapped between your upper left arm and chest. In the downswing, you will pull the glove across your chest and around it to the left.

DRILL 3: Club Across Shoulders

Hold a club across the front of your shoulders and assume your address position for the one-plane swing. Turn your shoulders fully, so that the club shaft points to the right of the ball and toward the outer half (the outside 24 inches) of the zone that runs from the ball to 48 inches outside the ball.

As you make this turn, your spine and head should drift slightly to the right (away from the target). Check in a mirror to see that this slight drift occurs. Return to address position and repeat several times.

PART 3

PERFECTING YOUR SLOT

By **JIM MCLEAN, PGA**
Jim McLean Golf School
Doral Golf Resort
Miami, Fla.
*1995 PGA Teacher
of the Year*

GOLF MAGAZINE
TOP 100 TEACHERS IN AMERICA

For more information on slotting the club and grooving a power-rich delivery not only with your driver, but also with your irons and wedges, check out **The Slot Swing** *(Wiley, $25.95)*. It's the only book ever written on the one move pros make and amateurs don't.

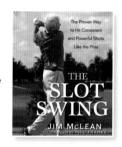

THE SLOT SWING
JIM McLEAN

ny swing when you drop the shaft from a higher backswing plane to a lower downswing plane is what I call a "slot swing." As I'm sure you've already gathered by reading this book, there are many different ways to slot your club to achieve the right delivery path. In my opinion, you only need to be familiar with two important elements that make any slot swing work:

1. Your shaft position flattens in your downswing and finds the most effective delivery line to the ball.

2. You change your shaft position by dropping into the Slot after you complete your backswing.

There are three ways to do this, which comprise the three slot swings covered in the following excerpt. (It'll be up to you to experiment with each and decide which is the best model for you to copy based on the information in this chapter as well as the previous). These swings share a common trait, in that they train you to change your downswing shaft position and achieve the power-rich delivery line featured in all high-level swings.

The slot position is the fundamental downswing key to hitting successful shots. When you find it, you have the best chance to release the club freely and generate solid contact, a penetrating ball flight, and the correct trajectory for the club you're holding in your hands. It's the perfect place from which to deliver a centered blow with speed via the correct angle of attack.

A perfect swing is one that repeats. It's one that is powerful and accurate and, most impor-

tant, works under pressure. That's why this book emphasizes finding your Slot more than it does finding perfect looking backswings. Making a perfect looking backswing doesn't mean you'll be perfect at impact. The proof is simple – just look at the greatest ball strikers in history. Examine the swings that have lasted. Think about the swings that stand the test of time. They all find the slot. Nevertheless, slot swings are designed to improve the swings of recreational golfers (i.e., you). Although I use professionals such as Sergio Garcia and Jim Furyk to demonstrate how

Pros swing a bit out on the way up and then slot the club so they attack the ball from the inside.

the slot works, it's still something the average weekend golfer can learn to improve his game.

As you read through this section, you'll discover how the simple moves that make up the act of slotting the club in your downswing can be. Plus, the Slot Swing eliminates the most damaging swing error you can make: coming over the top.

Coming over the top is a move made by many amateurs who visit my schools. Even as I watch players tee off on one of the courses here at Doral Golf Resort, I see mostly over-the-top swings. Very rarely will an amateur slot the club and approach the ball properly from inside the target line. But you can put an end to any chance of making this mistake in your swing right now by finding the best way for you to find the slot every single time.

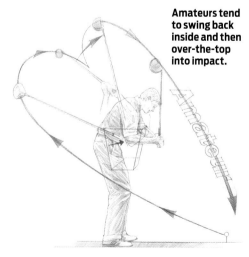

Amateurs tend to swing back inside and then over-the-top into impact.

The Slot Swing: How It Works

So far, I've mentioned the word plane several times. Specifically I've described the main element of the Slot Swing as a switch from a backswing plane to a flatter downswing plane. The question begs then, "What's the best plane?" Whenever I'm asked, I'm tempted to answer, "Delta" or "Continental," because there isn't one – at least, where your golf swing is concerned. Watch any professional tournament on TV, and you'll see in an instant that the ideal backswing plane differs from golfer to golfer. The concept gets really complicated when you consider that each of the clubs in your bag is built with a unique lie angle and that you swing them on different slopes.

If you're like most golfers, you're intimidated by plane. I don't blame you; discussions on the topic are vague and incomplete. Over the years, you've been misled by the oft-used illustration depicting swing plane as a shadowed area (typically a sheet of glass) that rests on your shoulders. Despite the good intentions of this graphic, it doesn't tell you anything about the plane on which you start your swing, just the one at the midpoint in your backswing (and mainly for your lead arm). Your swing begins on an, "address plane," defined by the angle formed by the shaft when you sole your clubhead on the ground. The address plane is many degrees flatter than the sheet of glass. Obviously, something has to happen in order for you to change from the lower

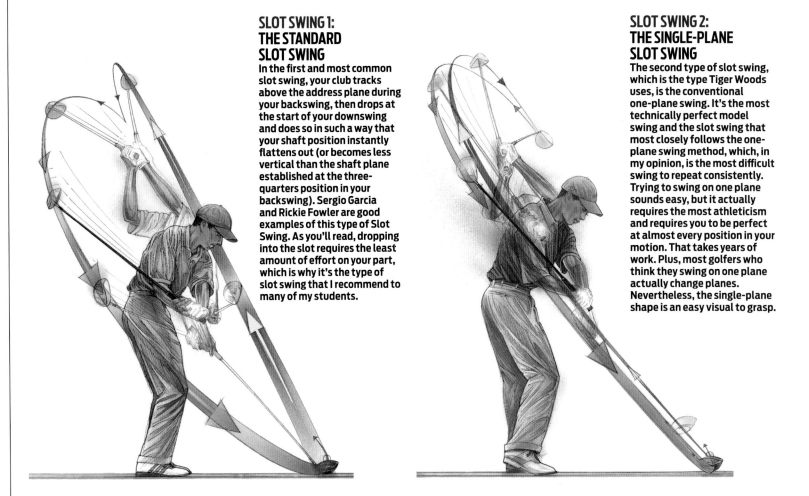

SLOT SWING 1:
THE STANDARD
SLOT SWING
In the first and most common slot swing, your club tracks above the address plane during your backswing, then drops at the start of your downswing and does so in such a way that your shaft position instantly flattens out (or becomes less vertical than the shaft plane established at the three-quarters position in your backswing). Sergio Garcia and Rickie Fowler are good examples of this type of Slot Swing. As you'll read, dropping into the slot requires the least amount of effort on your part, which is why it's the type of slot swing that I recommend to many of my students.

SLOT SWING 2:
THE SINGLE-PLANE
SLOT SWING
The second type of slot swing, which is the type Tiger Woods uses, is the conventional one-plane swing. It's the most technically perfect model swing and the slot swing that most closely follows the one-plane swing method, which, in my opinion, is the most difficult swing to repeat consistently. Trying to swing on one plane sounds easy, but it actually requires the most athleticism and requires you to be perfect at almost every position in your motion. That takes years of work. Plus, most golfers who think they swing on one plane actually change planes. Nevertheless, the single-plane shape is an easy visual to grasp.

address plane to the higher backswing plane as you power the club to the top.

The same goes for your downswing, but here you need to change from a higher plane to a lower plane. Often, when an amateur attempts this, he tries to track the move he made going back. That's not how it works. Your hands don't re-track on the way back down to the ball. They remain on the same plane they rest on at the top (or get slightly steeper). It's the clubshaft that falls to the lower plane (finds the slot), a move that happens naturally when you trigger your downswing by shifting your lower-body center toward the target.

It's important to realize that the act of swinging "on plane" doesn't mean that your hands, left arm, and shaft work in the same plane at the same time. Although there are some points in your swing where everything matches up, it's incredibly difficult to plane everything perfectly, including the clubhead, the shaft, the hands, and the arms. While it might look good on paper or to a scientist, achieving perfect positions is incredibly difficult and unnatural. It doesn't correspond to an athletic throwing motion or hitting mechanics. Trying to be perfect usually leads to over thinking, freezing up, and, at times, quitting the game.

The best thing about the Slot Swing is that it doesn't care about your exact backswing plane or backswing path. As you'll learn, it won't matter what plane you take as you swing the club to the top or what plane your club sits on when you get there. To make things easier I've built in several Safety Corridors that, in essence, demand that you simply get within a range. The only plane of extreme importance is the one you shift your clubshaft onto at the start of your downswing as you move toward impact.

SLOT SWING 3:
THE REVERSE-SLOT SWING

The third type of slot swing is a reverse of the first, which is why I call it the reverse-slot swing. The clubhead swings inside during the takeaway and under the shaft plane in a way that could be described as "flat." Reverse-slot swingers such as Sam Snead, J.B. Holmes, and Matt Kuchar are good examples. They make an early turn in the backswing and position the right arm and elbow well behind the body. Starting down, the hands and arms loop well outward to get everything lined up. The clubhead trails the hands, instead of tipping over in front of the body: a classic death move for many players.

THE REVERSE SLOT SWING: THE SLEDGEHAMMER

Although modern machinery has made the act of swinging a sledgehammer nearly obsolete, most people are familiar with the action. You've seen it dozens of times in movies and on TV—the laboring railroad worker driving a spike into a section of railroad track. Take away the railroad and the tumble weeds, and replace the sledgehammer with a driver or a 7-iron, and you have the Reverse Slot.

Because the hammer is heavy, the worker swings it inside, and once he gains momentum, he lifts it up using the big muscles in his shoulders and back. Think about how you move another heavy object, such as a beer keg. You tip it on its bottom edge and roll it. In other words, "you turn weight." That's the easiest and most natural way to move a heavy object.

In order to build momentum and really drive that spike into the rail, the man swinging the sledgehammer loops his hands up and over at the start of his downswing. This is precisely the move that a young junior makes when swinging a club that's a bit too heavy. Although his arms and hands loop out away from him, the head of the sledgehammer stays back. It trails the hands. The man driving the spike into the railroad tie never thinks about these moves, but he hits that spike dead center.

Think about this, would a person driving a spike be better off taking a sledgehammer straight up on a perfect plane and then tracing that perfect plane down to the spike? If that were true, don't you think they would have done it?

The secret to swinging in the Reverse Slot is probably to learn it at an early age. It is the most natural way to play golf, yet almost nobody talks about it or teaches it, which I think is a mistake.

The Secret To Finding the Slot

The fact that no two professionals look exactly alike at the top – but look so similar once they get halfway down to impact – gives you an idea of the power of the Slot and how it can fix unorthodox backswing positions so that the clubhead can approach the ball from the inside and transfer all the energy of your swing into the hit. It's also the power of your first moves down from the top, when the slot takes shape.

Although it's possible to hit good shots without finding the slot, it requires that you time an infinite number of bad motions and off-plane angles. This is difficult for most amateurs to do on a consistent basis, which explains why they often follow a good shot with a bad one. This type of inconsistency disappears when you learn to find the Slot during your downswing.

Regardless of what your top of the backswing position looks like, your lower body is the first thing to move from the top, and the principles involved in this motion are the same ones you use in every athletic throwing motion or hitting motion. These principles are shifting, rotating your body center, and releasing your right arm (for a right-handed golfer). You can't defy the laws of an athletic throw if your goal is to hit the ball far and straight. And once you apply them, you won't have to consciously think about pulling the club downward. (You may feel a pull in your left arm, but that'll only be in response to the force generated by your body turn. Correct body actions ensure that the arms whip the club powerfully into impact from inside so that the center of your clubface makes contact with the back of the ball).

This means that the first move down – the first act in slotting the club in your downswing – is a "below-the-belt" event. Almost immediately on finishing your backswing, get your lower body moving toward the target. Lee Trevino always said that he like to "break my knees toward the target" to start the downswing. That's one good way to capture the correct feel.

Drop down into the Slot and you won't be able to swing over the top.

Pulling the handle of the club down will help you find the Slot.

Three key Ways to Slot the Club

Your first move from the top is to shift your lower body laterally toward the target. As you shift your knees forward, moving your weight along with them, allow the triangle formed your elbows and arms to drop down. If you do it correctly, the clubshaft will be trailing and, due to the forward action of your lower body and soft wrist joints,

automatically flatten out and drop behind you.

Your arms react to your lower body moving toward the target. The leading action of your lower body causes a quick separation. Basically, you're trying to leave your arms and hands (as well as the club) behind. Causing your club to trail is what positions it in the slot. As your arms drop and your lower body moves forward, your clubshaft should flatten. It shifts onto a lower plane without your even having to think about it.

It should feel as if the clubshaft and the clubhead are falling behind your body. When I first instruct a student to drop down, however, he tends to pull hard with his left arm, a move that yanks the clubshaft in front of the body and destroys any chance of finding the slot. The secret is to drop your right elbow close to your hip and underneath your right hand. Done correctly, it should feel as if your right elbow is moving toward the ball. This is one of the key moves that flattens the shaft. Try it a few times while you are sitting. Even without a golf club, you can imagine the shaft flattening out as you execute this important move.

If you need something to focus on as you transition from backswing to downswing, key in on your right elbow. From the top, it should feel as if your right elbow is trying to get inside your right pants pocket. I call this position the "Hitters Pocket," with your right elbow in tight and the club behind your body. Once you're in the pocket, you're primed to deliver a powerful inside hit on the ball.

NOTE: it's important for you to understand that the force that reverses the swing's direction from back to forward comes first from the lower body and is relayed immediately to the upper body. The last this to change direction is the clubhead.

Every good ball-striker sets the club into the Slot and gets his right elbow in close to the body. As long as your shaft flattens into this acceptable zone, your ball-striking will improve. From here, it's impossible to swing over the top.

The action of skipping a stone off the lake is the same motion your right arm makes in the Slot

DRILL #1: ROCK TOSS

Grab a golf ball in your right hand, stand at ease, and swing your right arm back. Now try to throw the ball as if you're skipping a stone off a lake. Since you didn't establish an athletic base to begin your throw, you may have to think twice about how to get your right arm in action and sling it in a somewhat sidearm move so that the ball will skip. The correct way to do it is start your lower body moving forward and pull your right elbow into your right side. If you make these moves fast enough, your right wrist will bend back and you'll feel your right forearm actually move back at the same time that your right elbow moves forward. Once this happens, release your right forearm past your body by straightening your right elbow.

Practicing from a closed stance and visualizing an inside approach trains you to trace an inside path to the ball.

DRILL #2: FIGURE EIGHT

Address the ball with any club. As you look down, picture an imaginary figure eight on the ground, with the top of the eight pointing at the target. (If you can draw the figure eight on the grass, even better. Just check with your superintendent firrst). You can also draw the eight with chalk in your garage or driveway.)

Start with small, slow motion swings. From your address, swing the clubhead over the outside half of the eight. When you reach the top, use the eight to remind yourself to loop the club to the inside and then approach the ball from inside the target line on your downswing. Continue to trace the eight past impact so that the clubhead exits in an arc through the hitting zone and eventually moves left of the target. Repeat until the move becomes natural.

Tracing an imaginary figure eight captures the essence of the Slot: an outside takeaway, a loop at the top, and an inside approach.

DRILL #3: HIT SOME DRAWS

Set up to the ball with any club and picture a clock on the ground, with the ball in the middle of the face and the 12 pointing toward the target. Make your Slot Swing, but this time focus on swinging the clubhead over the 7 as you approach the ball and over the 1 after contact. If this is difficult for you, address the ball with a slightly closed stance (right foot pulled back from the target line). Now hit the inside quadrant of the golf ball. This drill teaches you to approach the ball from inside the target line—a mainstay of the Slot Swing. You are almost forced to loop the club to the inside attack track. It's the only way to hit the ball way out to the right of your stance line on a consistent basis and also a great way to kill your slice.

5 THINGS TO TAKE FROM THIS CHAPTER

1 Your best swing is locked inside of you. Take the tests to discover your most natural way to swing the club to the top and then back down.

2 The shape, speed, torque and delivery of your swing is defined for you and you alone. Spend the time refining it to get the most out of it.

3 The folding action of your right elbow elevates the club to the shoulder plane on each and every swing you make. You can deliver the club from there or drop to a lower plane. This drop is the act of slotting.

4 One- and 2-plane swings are more about how your upper body and lower body turn in relation to each other and the most efficient ways to create max speed.

5 Perfecting your best swing is best done by performing drills that help you groove your motion in full.

3-POST/HIGH-MID SLOT DRIVER
DUSTIN JOHNSON

His downward slot has potentially cost him two majors

At 6' 4", Dustin Johnson has the perfect physique to deliver power through a graceful motion that features a ton of leverage. Without a few final-round disasters he'd already be a two-time major winner, but as is the case with most players who slot away from their natural track like Johnson does, inconsistency and round-wrecking swings can pop up without notice.

Johnson has a beautifully controlled swing that produces powerful clubhead speed. He tracks back effortlessly [*Frame 3*], hitting his shoulder plane with ease (his thumb is way above his right shoulder in the Elbow Test).

At the top he bows his left wrist noticeably, shutting the clubface. This doesn't set him up for a hook, but rather allows him to swing down as fast as he can without worrying about rotating the clubface to square as much as open- or square-face players.

Coming down he tucks his right elbow to slot the club to his right-arm plane [*Frame 8*]. This seems like a power move, but it may be a little to severe. Notice how he must move his legs laterally and slightly rise up out of his address posture [*Frame 13*] in order to fight off the centrifugal forces that would otherwise flip the club to the left. For Johnson, the technique works, but it can't—and won't—hold up under pressure like a pure rotary motion (track-to-track).

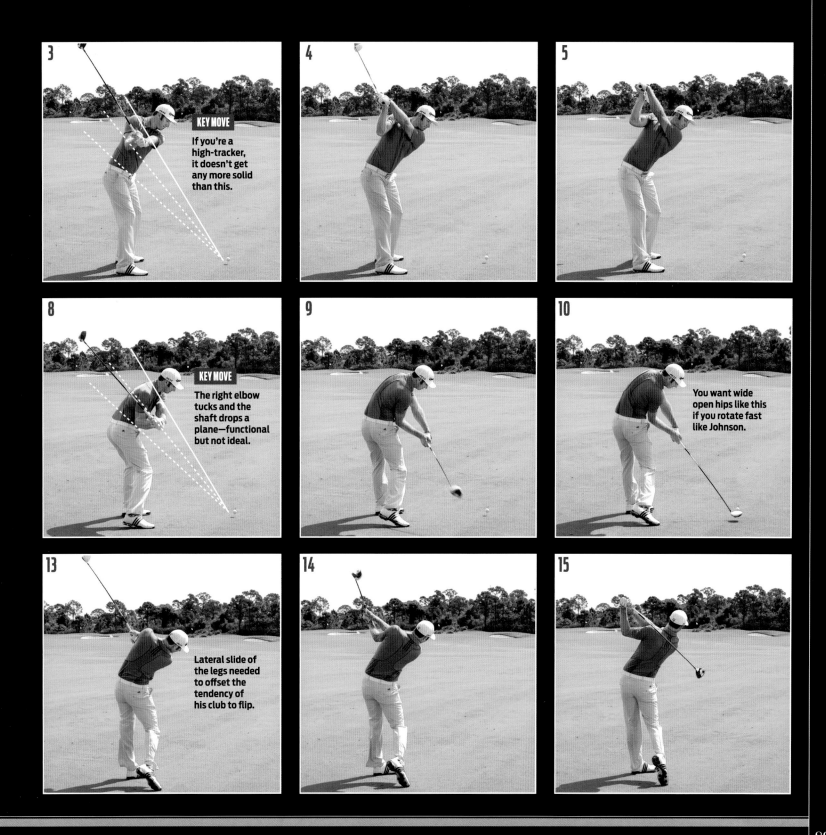

3

KEY MOVE
If you're a high-tracker, it doesn't get any more solid than this.

4

5

8

KEY MOVE
The right elbow tucks and the shaft drops a plane—functional but not ideal.

9

10

You want wide open hips like this if you rotate fast like Johnson.

13

Lateral slide of the legs needed to offset the tendency of his club to flip.

14

15

CHAPTER 5

There are other options, but a neutral clubface is typically best for most amateurs.

THE FINE *ART* OF CLUBFACE CONTROL

At impact your driver can be square, open or closed. Here's how to control it from start to finish for flush hits every time you swing.

By **DR. JIM SUTTIE, PGA**
*TwinEagles Club
Naples, Fla.*

*2000 PGA Teacher
of the Year*

GOLF
MAGAZINE
TOP 100
TEACHERS
IN AMERICA

AS YOU'RE LEARNING AS YOU READ through this book, there are as many ways to swing your driver as there are people doing it. Even the very best tee-ball hitters have quirks in their motions that make them a bit different from the rest, but they all know how to time their swing and square the clubface at the point of impact. This commonality among accomplished players is very real and it cannot be disputed. Whether you're one-plane, two-plane, or a center-poster with medium-speed hips, it's imperative that you get your clubface pointing in the same direction as your clubhead path when you strike the ball (unless you're purposely shaping a shot to the left or right). And this can't happen once in a while. A square clubface is a must every time you hit a drive. The more you can repeat the position, the better you'll be.

The manner in which you square the clubface is much like the manner in which you swing your driver to the top of your backswing and then back through the ball. By that I mean it *depends*, specifically on your physical factors (body build, flexibility, muscle tension, natural power, balance, etc.), psychological and emotional factors ("this position feels wrong to me"), your natural swing pattern, and how much knowledge you have about your swing. You must consider each and every one of these factors when constructing your face-squaring method. However, it's important to realize that you'll adjust your swing and the way you move your body in response to what your clubface is doing when you swing. In a sense, the position of your clubface at every point in your motion controls you. This makes the clubface the king, and selects you as either a square-, shut-, or open-face golfer. In this chapter I'll describe how to determine if you're a candidate for each one and the ways to control the clubface so it's in position when you need it the most—impact.

As you process the material on the following pages, keep in mind that the method you've been using to this point in your golfing career can significantly affect your ability to change methods. For example, if you've been hitting shots with a closed clubface for the last twenty years, you obviously will have a hard time going all the way to an open clubface, and vice versa. And if your body isn't very flexible and you've been hitting the ball with a lot of hand action for a long time, it will be a stretch to begin hitting with quiet hands and lots of body rotation. This is why I would recommend that anyone who wants to drive the ball more consistently consider becoming more neutral in their delivery of the clubface to the ball. It's the method that requires the fewest compensations and the greatest potential for consistency.

Regardless of how you currently hit the ball, the good news is, you can get better. Match the proper delivery method to your physical capabilities and grip preference and you'll be well on the way to hitting more fairways.

FIRST STEPS: Square, Open or Closed?

Golf terminology is often confusing and misleading. When you hear someone say, "Keep the clubface square through impact," what does he mean? Square to what? Another example: "You're shut at the top." Shut from what? Here's what square, closed and open really mean:

SQUARE: Your clubface is pointing in the direction of your clubhead path.

CLOSED: Your clubface is pointing to the left of your clubhead path. This also is referred to as shut.

OPEN: Your clubface is pointing to the right of your clubhead path.

The important thing is that these terms don't apply to a single position or moment in time. Your clubface position can be constantly changing at every moment in your motion, or maintain its arrangement relative to the clubhead path from start to finish. The key thing to remember is that it's perfectly okay to stray

"The position of your clubface at every point in your motion controls you. This makes it the king, and selects you as either a square-, shut-, or open-face golfer."

A clubface that's parallel to the target line at the top of your backswing is square (or neutral). This is arguably the most reliable position from which to hit straight shots.

from square during your motion if that's the best way for you to swing. That's why, despite the millions of different ways to swing your driver, there are only three ways to strike the ball: With a square clubface, a closed (shut) clubface or an open clubface. Despite what method you use, however, your clubface—as demonstrated by James Leitz in Chapter 1—needs to be square to your clubhead path (pointing in the same direction where your clubhead is moving) or you'll suffer from an unwanted direction and curve.

Classic Notes on Clubface Position

In their ground-breaking 1968 book *Search for the Perfect Swing*, Alistair Cochran and John Stobbs wrote, "All golfers, in fact, 'roll the clubhead.' They have to, in order to swing it from a position where it lies at about 90° to the swing's plane and arc as it faces the hole at the address, to a position where it lies end to end within, or parallel to the plane at the top of the backswing; and then again in order to swing it back again through that 90°

> ## "Despite the millions of ways to swing your driver, there are only three ways to strike a ball: With a square clubface, a closed (shut) clubface or an open clubface."

angle during the final stages of the downswing. Only about 30% of the clubhead roll to the top is a result of the 'wrist roll,' or more accurately, rotation of the left forearm. The other 60% is a result from a combination of arm raising and shoulder training."

The lesson: Opening and closing the clubface, depending on which method you use, is a whole-body event and not a simple twist of your hands and wrists. Thus, performing the method you choose should feel natural, not forced. If you find yourself struggling in any way, experiment with the other two positions. You'll know pretty quick if the new technique works better than your old one—your drives will fly straighter.

A VISUAL LOOK AT THE THREE SQUARING METHODS

SQUARE-FACE METHOD
The clubface points in the direction of the swing arc or clubhead path from start to finish. To do this, it must rotate as the clubhead traces its circular path up and back down, and you rotate it with your wrists, arms and shoulders.

SHUT-FACE METHOD
The clubface points to the left of the swing arc or clubhead path as it approaches impact, reaching a square position at impact with less rotation.

OPEN-FACE METHOD
The clubface points to the right of the swing arc or clubhead path as it approaches impact because it was rotated significantly in the backswing. An active closing of the clubface through impact is necessary to catch the ball square.

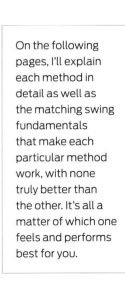

On the following pages, I'll explain each method in detail as well as the matching swing fundamentals that make each particular method work, with none truly better than the other. It's all a matter of which one feels and performs best for you.

 Jim Suttie shows you each method in a video lesson at **golf.com/bestdriving book**

Three Ways to Control the Clubface

How to choose the clubface-squaring method that's right for you

SQUARE-FACE METHOD

This technique employs a square clubface throughout, or one that's perpendicular to the arc of your clubhead path as you swing back and then down.

CHECKPOINT 1: At the Top
The clubface is tilted at a 45-degree angle with the leading edge sitting parallel to your left wrist and forearm [*left*].

CHECKPOINT 2: Halfway Down
At about the time the shaft gets back to parallel to the ground, the toe of your club should point straight at the sky, and your clubface should point perpendicularly to your target line with the leading edge in line with your hands [*below*].

PGA Tour Examples: *Ernie Els, Steve Stricker, Greg Norman*

SHUT-FACE METHOD

This technique employs a closed clubface, or one that points to the left of the arc of your clubhead as you swing back and then down.

HOW YOU KNOW IT'S RIGHT FOR YOU

- You have medium hip speed [*see page 44*].
- You like to keep things neutral in your swing—compensations are not welcome!
- You naturally move your best when you feel like your upper and lower bodies are working together.
- You prefer a smooth tempo over a fast or slow one.
- You feel most comfortable with a neutral grip.
- You tend to hit the ball fairly straight most of the time.

HOW YOU KNOW IT'S RIGHT FOR YOU

- You have fast hips [*see page 44*].
- You're flexible and capable of making a big shoulder turn.
- You fight a slice or tend to hit the ball too high.
- Your swing feels more dynamic and powerful the more you use your legs.
- You prefer a fast tempo over a smooth or slow one.
- You feel most comfortable with a strong grip.

I'm demonstrating with an oversized iron to make it easier to see where the clubface is actually pointing.

CHECKPOINT 1: At the Top

The clubface is pointing at the sky with the leading edge near parallel to the ground. Your left wrist is bowed with your left elbow directly underneath the clubhead [*left*].

CHECKPOINT 2: Halfway Down

At about the time the shaft gets back to parallel to the ground, the toe of your club is ahead of your hands with your clubface already pointing toward the ground. If you attached a flashlight to the clubface the light would shine on the ball [*below*].

PGA Tour Examples: *Dustin Johnson, Rickie Fowler, Graeme McDowell*

OPEN-FACE METHOD

This technique employs an open clubface, or one that points to the right of the arc of your clubhead as you swing back and then down.

HOW YOU KNOW IT'S RIGHT FOR YOU

- You have slow or mid-speed hips [*see page 44*].
- You're inflexible or don't turn as well as you used to.
- You're okay with sacrificing some distance for a little extra accuracy off the tee.
- You're a "feel" player and prefer an arm-driven or "handsy" swing.
- You prefer a smooth or even a slower tempo.
- You prefer a neutral or weak grip.

CHECKPOINT 1: At the Top

The clubface is pointing away from you (near perpendicular to your target line) with the toe hanging straight down. Your left wrist is cupped and your elbows feel like they're far apart [*left*].

CHECKPOINT 2: Halfway Down

Here, the toe of your club is behind your hands and points behind you, while the clubface is pointing more toward the sky—you could check the time on a wristwatch if you were wearing one on your left hand [*below*].

PGA Tour Examples: *Fred Couples, Brian Gay, Mark Calcavecchia*

Creating a Balance Between Accuracy and Distance

As courses get tighter and longer, both distance and direction off the tee have become increasingly important considerations. Some golfers choose to take the distance route, adding power features to their swings to get as many yards out of it as possible. Others opt for a higher dosage of accuracy fundamentals. It's a slippery slope, however, if and when you start favoring one driving parameter over the other.

For example, PGA Tour players Bubba Watson and Dustin Johnson do a fantastic job of tapping their physical builds to hit the ball 300 yards and longer almost every time they swing. Raw power, however, has come with a hefty price tag for these two popular players [*see table, below*]. On the flip side, two of the most accurate drivers on today's Tour, Brian Gay and Heath Slocum, rank near the bottom of the distance stat column.

PLAYER	Driving Distance (Rank)	Driving Accuracy (Rank)
Dustin Johnson	301.1 yds. (4th)	57.2% (127th)
Bubba Watson	310.8 yds. (2nd)	60.7% (94th)
Brian Gay	269.9 yds. (183rd)	75.2% (1st)
Heath Slocum	276.8 yds (166th)	70.3% (6th)

Data courtesy ShotLink. Through 2011 Memorial Tournament

Yes, golf is a power game, but accuracy and distance control are paramount if you want to score your best. The best scenario is to generate good distance *and* direction, which makes choosing the method with which you square the clubface critical. Each provides its own unique blend of power and accuracy. All of them are equally efficient—the shut-face style is just as effective as the open-face style. It all depends on who's using it.

If one part of your driving game is suffering while the other is in decline (like any of the Tour examples listed above), it's a good idea to get your clubface back to neutral—a base position that you can better control and from which you can add extra power or accuracy (depending on your personal taste and the conditions in which you typically play). Therein lies the benefit of the square-face motion. It's a simple method that keeps everything neutral so that compensations can be held to a minimum. Again, I can't recommend which style you should use because it needs to match your fundamentals, and I don't know what those are. I can only offer suggestions. If you're really struggling off the tee, however, the square-face method and its inherent neutrality is a good place to start.

How to Make a Square-Face Swing

The hallmark setup traits of the square-face method are a neutral grip and a neutral swing, and that no one body part is doing more work than the others. Because of this compensations are minimal—always a good thing. When it goes right the square-face swing looks like everything is working together in total synchronization. For that reason it requires an even, smooth tempo.

To test this method, set up as neutral as you can and feel like your lower and upper bodies are working in tandem from start to finish. Stay aggressive, but don't add any quick movements or spasms to your motion, and make sure you hit the following five keys.

KEY No.1

Neutral Grip
Point the "Vs" on both hands at your chin.

KEY No.2

Set the Face
Set the leading edge of your clubhead parallel with your left arm. Don't flex or cup your left wrist. Feel like the triangle created by your forearms is supporting the club.

KEY No. 3

Sync Up

Make an even swing coming down—don't allow your lower body to race out ahead or spin out with your shoulders from the top. You know you're doing it right if your clubface points perpendicularly to the target line halfway down.

KEY No. 4

Straight-Line Impact

Line up everything—left arm, shaft, clubhead, left hip—at impact and at the same time.

KEY No. 5

Diagonal Release

Release the club diagonally and in the same plane as your forearms. Feel like you're swinging out to left-centerfield on a baseball diamond.

"The square-face swing looks like everything is working together in total sync."

How to Make A Shut-Face Swing

Some of the best drivers in the game (both past and present) are shut-faced players. Key to their technique is limiting the amount that they roll their forearms and wrists, which keeps the clubface from opening. In fact, the clubface actually closes it in relation to the path as the swing traces its arc. This fact alone makes the shut-face method the easiest to time. The caveat is that you must be in top physical shape in order to swing this way because it demands more body action than hand and arm action. If you ever get handsy in your swing while employing the shut-face technique you'll hit a nasty hook. That's why you see hut-face players aim up the right side of the fairway.

KEY No. 1

Strong Grip

Rotate your hands to the right. Gripping the club this way restricts your ability to rotate your forearms on your backswing and downswing. It also helps you "hold off" at impact and stop your hands from taking over and whipping the ball left. Generally, but not always, shut-face player stay away from taking an open stance—they aim where they don't want to go and swing to where they want to go.

KEY No. 2

Big Shoulder Turn

Because you limit the role your arms and hands play in your swing, you limit the speed and power they add to open- and square-face swings. You must make up for it by turning your shoulders as far as you can on your backswing and create as much potential energy as possible. This is why shut-face players tend to be the most flexible. You know you're in correct position at the top if your clubface points toward the sky.

KEY No. 3

Downswing Leg Drive

The hips not only must move forward, but also rotate more than 60 degrees on your downswing in order to deliver the clubhead properly and to make up for the loss of speed from your hands. At the same time, your right shoulder must work down and underneath to offset this aggressive turn. The combination can be very hard on your back if you're not in peak physical condition.

KEY No. 4

Passive Hands at Impact

Keep your hands quiet through the hitting zone. I like to think of shut-face impact as "shoving" the ball toward your target rather than hitting through it. I call it a "push-shove" impact because you need to get your left hand out in front of the clubhead (shaft leaning toward the target) at impact or the ball will hook.

KEY No. 5

Vertical Release
A vertical release is critical. If you release the club to the left of the target line, you're toast. Instead, feel like you're swinging out to right field on a baseball diamond. Keep your left arm long (don't bend it) and make sure your left-hand knuckles are pointing at the sky.

SHUT-FACE SWING PROS & CONS
The shut-faced method is a legitimate way to become a great driver of the ball, but as mentioned previously, it requires that you be in good physical shape with a lot of hand and arm strength in order to hold off the centrifugal release of the clubhead through the ball. Another word of warning: This method is very hard on your back and your left wrist, shoulder and elbow. The trade off is that it makes hitting the ball straight much easier.

SHUT PROS	SHUT CONS
Better accuracy	Physically demanding
Easier to time	Requires strength & flexibility
Less hand manipulation	More lower-body action

How to Make An Open-Face Swing

Unlike the shut-face method, which uses the body as the main power source, the open-face method taps the hands and arms. This may seem like a sure-fire way to rob your swing of power, but in many cases amateurs hit the ball farther because the significant closing action need to get the clubface square at impact actually adds to overall clubhead speed. It's also a good technique for amateurs because it doesn't require as much flexibility. The secret to making it work is forearm and wrist rotation—and lots of it. Basically you're looking to open the clubface on your backswing by turning your wrists and forearms to the right and then reversing the process as you swing into impact.

KEY No. 1

Set Up Your Hand Action

Grip the club with a slightly weak grip—get that "V" formed between your thumbs and forefingers pointed at your left shoulder. A weaker grip releases the tension in your wrists so that you can rotate them to the right freely during your backswing. You need this rotation to both open the clubface and to create speed on your downswing (by rotating your wrists and arms in the opposite direction through impact).

KEY No. 2

Full Torque Turn

If you can turn your shoulders, great, but the open-face method doesn't require that you have to, which is why it's a great option for players with back pain and/or limited flexibility. Don't be so concerned with torquing your upper body against your lower. Turn both your hips and your shoulders as far as you can, but use your wrist and forearm rotation to swing the club back and get the toe pointing toward the ground at the top.

KEY No. 3

Go Slow and Then Hit

The good news with this swing method is that you don't have to go at the ball hard with your lower body. Start your downswing by turning, but then feel like your lower body suddenly stops and your hands and arms immediately take over. You must be aggressive with your hand action—picture your hands rapidly changing the clubface from open to closed as you're approaching the ball.

KEY No. 4

On Top Impact

Because you're using your hands to square the clubface you need to be more on top of the ball with your upper body at impact. If you hang back with this hand action you'll hit a very nasty high hook. A good way to stay on top is to keep your right hip high through impact. As you do this, try to get the toe of the club to contact the ball before the heel.

KEY No. 5

Full Release

If you don't make a full release with your right hand on top of your left in your follow-through, then it's an indication that you didn't square the face all the way at impact. The ball is going right. The best move you can make to ensure a full release is to keep your left elbow in close as you swing through the ball and then let it gently fold as you swing into your finish. You know you're doing it correctly if you feel the clubshaft swinging to the left of your target line in your forward-swing.

OPEN-FACE SWING PROS & CONS

In my opinion, the weekend golfer fares better with the open-faced driving method because it allows him or her to produce sufficient speed without relying on big turns and leg drives. The problem is that accuracy might suffer because of the excessive opening and closing of the clubface. Regardless, this is a very legitimate way to get good with your driver and to instill a better overall rhythm and tempo in your motion. ●

5 THINGS TO TAKE FROM THIS CHAPTER

1 The manner in which you square the clubface at impact depends on your swing style as well as your physical strengths and limitations.

2 It's important to strive for distance and accuracy in equal amounts, and not favor one too much over the other.

3 There are three ways to motion your clubface as you swing: square, open and closed.

4 The square method is the most neutral of the three and should be used as a base when experimenting with this component of your technique.

5 Don't attempt a method if it doesn't play to your strengths.

OPEN PROS	OPEN CONS
Speed gain (amateurs)	Potential loss of accuracy
Requires less athletic ability	Speed loss (pros)
Builds rhythm and timing	Mistime it and the ball is going right

Special thanks to instruction model Paul Park.

MID-TRACK/MID-SPEED DRIVER
ADAM SCOTT

If you want to hit it as straight as
you do long, this is your swing

1

2

Long drives usually result from swinging under control. They're more about rhythm and timing than anything else, and while Adam Scott is often pegged as a "go-for-the-fences" driver, he actually swings very smoothly and with a lot of neutral (i.e., easy to control) angles in his motion. This has helped him reach nearly the very top of the PGA Tour's Total Driving stat category.

Scott is a mid-track golfer with a picture-perfect takeaway that initially sets the club outside his hands [*Frame 2*] and then perfectly in line with his hands [*Frame 3*] with a neutral clubface position (notice how the clubface points perpendicularly to his target line). His erect posture at address, however, causes him to track above his natural right-arm plane.

After setting the club and rising up to the shoulder plane, Scott starts back down with a smooth, unhurried pace (he has medium hip speed). In past interviews, Scott has stated that he doesn't want too much going on from the waist down. If your hips outrace everything, then you'll probably miss the fairway.

He drops back down to his natural plane and is so synced up that almost every position in his downswing is a carbon-copy of the same position in his backswing (compare Frames 3 and 10). With this kind of balance, Scott will continue to hit it deep and straight for a very long time.

6

Rises above
shoulder plane.
He'd track on his
right arm back
and through with
better posture.

7

Neutral face
position at the
top requires
less timing to
square it at
the bottom.

11

KEY MOVE

Looks can be
deceiving—
this ball is
going to go a
very long way.

12

3

4

Tracks above his natural plane due to poor (too erect) posture at address.

5

8

9

KEY MOVE

Smoothly drops back to his natural tracking plane.

10

Totally synced up with the clubhead perfectly square and in line with his hands.

13

14

15

CHAPTER

6

Driving for distance requires a combination of mobility, strength and speed. A golf-specific physical assessment is key to unlocking your power potential.

HOW TO FIND AND *MAXIMIZE* YOUR POWER

Learning what produces power in your swing—and then maximizing it by understanding how your body works—is the proven method to add extra yards off the tee

By **DAVE PHILLIPS, PGA**
Titleist Performance Institute, Oceanside, Calif.

I WEAR TWO DIFFERENT HATS TO work every day: One for my role as a PGA teaching professional, and another as cofounder of the Titleist Performance Institute (TPI), launched by the equipment company of the same name in 2004. The duality of my work and, more important, *where* I work allow me to look at, research and understand the game in a way very few instructors are able. The Institute is more than just another high-tech lesson tee. It's an Olympic-style training center that looks at every aspect of performance. TPI is so advanced that the players who train here (a steady stream of golfers from every professional tour and juniors and amateurs who want to achieve their individual goals) often refer to it as the "Mayo Clinic of golf." At TPI we investigate golfers' techniques using 3D biomechanics, conduct physical and mental evaluations and extensively evaluate equipment—anything and everything that can potentially help players at all skill levels improve their games. As we've learned more about the swing and—as it relates to this book—how the best players in the world create power within it, our focus has shifted predominantly to these areas as a means to heighten performance. This has led to the creation of a philosophy at TPI that's really quite simple:

We don't believe there's one way to swing the club. We believe there are thousands of ways to swing the club, but that there's only one efficient way for you based on what you can physically do.

Many of the authors in this book have already touched on this philosophy—that your best swing is basically chosen for you. This isn't as constricting as it sounds because, like the philosophy states, there are thousands of "best swings" in the overall pool. My goal in this chapter is to make you more aware of your body and give you an understanding of your power sources and how to use them, i.e., hitting your drives as far as you possibly can. The secret, as you'll learn, is to locate the source of your swing power residing inside of you and exploit it. This, however, is impossible to do until you learn how and why the source affects the shape and overall action of your motion.

Golf is a game of speed, and creating the maximum amount of it requires that you establish certain positions in your swing and create movements in the correct sequence [*see Chapter 7*]. When you do this correctly, your swing speed rockets off the charts (and plummets like a lead balloon when you don't). This chapter is chock-full of terms like speed, strength, balance, stability and mobility. It's important that you become familiar with them. They're the power sources I touched on earlier that you'll need to maximize in order to play your best and hit the ball as far as possible, and they all relate to the most important piece of equipment you own—your body.

THE ESSENCE OF POWER

Swing power comes in all shapes, sizes and ages. For proof, look no further than Jamie Sadlowski [*photo, right*], the two-time Re/Max World Long Drive champion who stands but 5' 10" and weighs only 165 pounds, yet is able to generate over 150 mph of clubhead speed and in excess of 200 mph of ball speed (some of the fastest speeds ever recorded). Then there's long-drive competitor Domenic Mazza, who at the tender age of 16 routinely produces drives 400 yards and longer. Finally, 2010 Re/Max World Long Drive champion Joe Miller, the European long-drive record holder at 474 yards. Miller is six inches taller and 110 pounds heavier than Sadlowski.

An quick eyeball test crowns Miller the easy winner in a fictional three-man event, but the fact they compete at the same level simply proves that power is blind. Moreover, it's out there waiting for you—you just have to know where to find it. Players like Sadlowski, Mazza and Miller are able to produce prodigious length off the tee because they tap all of their individual power sources and the singular moves needed to maximize them. Sadlowski, for example, uses his freakish mobility to make an enormous backswing shoulder turn and get his hands high above his head while hinging his wrists to the max [*see sequence, page 116*]. Because of his combination of mobility, speed and strength he's able to hold his wrist angles deep into his downswing and then—POW! Joe Miller and Jason Zuback, another long-drive legend, tap a different power source. They employ more of a vertical "jump" and use ground-reaction forces to generate speed. Two completely different—yet effective—ways of creating power.

Power—Is It in You?
Wind back the clock and look back to your child-

Adding mobility is one way to generate speed and extra distance.

hood. I'm asking you to do this so that you can determine your level of activity when you were in your "speed window," the critical period(s) in your development as a child when you responded the fastest to a training stimulus. These windows typically occur in ages 5 to 8 and 12 to 15 for boys, and 4 to 7 and 10 to 12 for girls—ages when you're basically wired for speed. (The quick response

time is due to many factors, including hormonal influences, strength development, nervous system development and muscle fiber differentiation, among others). Child development research is very clear that if you trained like an athlete during your childhood (you threw, struck, kicked, jumped, ran, etc.), then it's likely that you maximized your speed window and still have some of that rocket fuel left over—natural speed you can use well into your adult life.

The bad news is that if you didn't do anything athletic during your speed windows then you're not hard wired for speed. Although you may never have the rocket fuel of someone who exploited their window, you certainly have plenty of jet fuel if you engaged in an athletic lifestyle after the age of 21—and there are some pretty fast jets. In the case that you were never athletic as a child or as an adult, you can forget about rockets and jets and instead focus on improving your flexibility and coordination—basically, go back to being a kid.

Understanding What Your Body Can Do
Now that you've learned a little bit about your body, the next step is to see what your body can actually do—how you're still able to put the jet or rocket fuel (your childhood athleticism) to

good use. Most of you probably wish to use it by swinging like the big hitters on Tour, or the long-drive competitors I've already mentioned. The problem is that you can't go to the range and simply copy their motions without putting yourself at risk for injury. For example, if you want to generate a bigger swing arc and get your arms high up in the air like Rory McIlroy or Dustin Johnson, then you need great shoulder range of motion and a hefty amount of lat flexibility [*see Chapter 8 to test your range of motion*]. If you don't have these attributes, then trying to mimic your idols is next to impossible without undue manipulation (and by creating swing faults or injuries). The same goes if you want to fire your hips through the ball and rotate your torso like Hunter Mahan or Tiger Woods. These moves require a substantial range of motion in your hips and the ability to separate your upper body from your lower. If you lack these qualities then you'll probably end up turning as a unit and come

down too steep and, again, putting yourself at risk for injury.

The point is that you probably aren't capable of copying what you see on TV because you're not physically capable of doing it. The fact that you even attempt to indicates that you're not fully in touch with your inherent strengths and limitations. In my opinion, the fastest way to increase your power is to understand what you can physically do, and work with a PGA professional to build a swing that matches your physical makeup. The series of tests Mike Adams presents in Chapter 3 is critical to discovering the type of swing style that best fits your body type. At TPI, we complement assessments such as this with a purely physical screening to see how we can make your style more powerful. Our screenings are performed by staff experts who run players through a variety of simple physical tests. They only take about 10 minutes to complete (you'll have a good time doing it, too).

TPI PHYSICAL SCREENING
WWW.MYTPI.COM

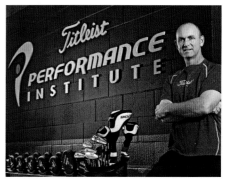

Here's your chance to improve what your body can do with a TPI-certified professional

In my opinion, you can't take any worthwhile steps toward improving your driving power and your overall game unless you get physically evaluated and understand what your body is capable of doing when you swing. Follow the directions below to take advantage of special offers with our nationwide network of TPI-certified professionals and learn more about your body and how it relates to your motion than every before, plus why you continue to make the same mistakes over and over.

HOW TO SCHEDULE YOUR ASSESSMENT

1. Go to **www.mytpi.com**.
2. Select the "Find an Expert" tab on the left side of the screen.
3. Type in your zip code or click your state to locate an expert who can help you reach your power and swing potential.
4. Mention *The Best Driving Instruction Book Ever!* when you make your appointment to receive special offers (where available) for a TPI physical evaluation.

 Dave Phillips walks you through the TPI screening experience at **golf.com/bestdrivingbook**

**Dustin Johnson
Copying his high-hands position only works if you have the shoulder mobility to handle it.**

**Hunter Mahan
Turning aggressively through impact like this requires core strength and a high level of hip mobility— amateur golfer beware!**

POWER KEY 1: MOBILITY

For obvious reasons, mobility in your swing is a benefit. But too much mobility can be just as much of a liability as too little. That's because mobility isn't a universal concept within your body. Some of your joints—your ankles are good examples—are designed to be highly mobile. Others—like those in your feet—are designed to be stable during movement.

According to strength and conditioning expert Mike Boyle and renowned physical therapist Grey Cook, your body is designed to operate in a pattern of stable segments connected to mobile joints [*photo, below*]. Even more interesting is that the pattern alternates: Joints that require greater mobility are surrounded above and below by joints that require greater stability, and vice versa. If at any time this pattern is broken, power loss and injury can occur. Think of a slingshot. You create elastic energy (torque) by stretching the band (a mobile joint), but the system only works if the mobile joint is stabilized, i.e. resisting with the handle.

Mobility: Creates elastic energy.
Stability: Creates balance, strength and endurance.

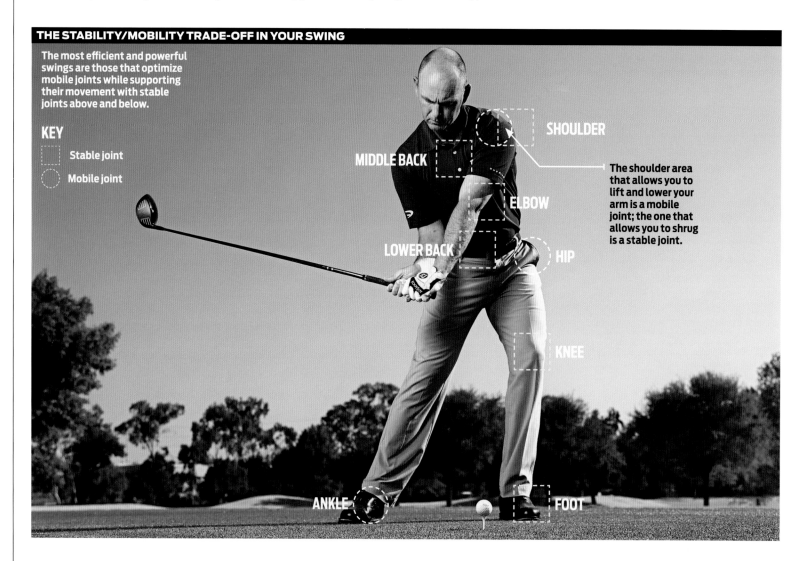

THE STABILITY/MOBILITY TRADE-OFF IN YOUR SWING

The most efficient and powerful swings are those that optimize mobile joints while supporting their movement with stable joints above and below.

KEY
☐ Stable joint
○ Mobile joint

SHOULDER

MIDDLE BACK

The shoulder area that allows you to lift and lower your arm is a mobile joint; the one that allows you to shrug is a stable joint.

ELBOW

LOWER BACK

HIP

KNEE

ANKLE

FOOT

How Mobile are You?

Here's an easy way to check if you have a mobility limitation. Stand in a tall posture with your arms by your sides (palms facing up) and your head facing forward. Without disturbing your posture or turning your head, rotate your upper body as far as you can to the left and right. As you turn in each direction pay attention to where you feel any tension in your body. Everyone feels tension (you may sense it as pressure) somewhere with this exercise—hips, lats, neck, etc. Where you sense it is a potential lack of mobility in that area, and a part of your body that needs addressing.

Sensing pressure or tightness in any area of your body as you make simple turns to the left and right indicates an area that's not as mobile as it should be, and a potential cause for a lack of distance and injury.

The Problem with Mobility Limitations

Having a mobility limitation saps your ability to create power. For example, if in the test above you felt tension in your hips and in your middle back, then you may have difficulty turning your upper body against the resistance of your lower body like most instructors advocate. Instead, you'll compensate by using a segment of your body that's meant to be stable like it's one that's meant to be mobile. This is why most common injuries occur in areas like the lower back, shoulders (scapula area), elbows and knees. Injury can occur by forcing a stable joint to move in a way it's not designed because you compensate for a lack of mobility in an area that's meant to be mobile.

The good news is that there are many methods which will enable you to play golf even with mobility limitations (seek the advice of Roger Fredericks and Jon Tattersall in Chapter 8).

However, unless you physically work out your mobility limitations you'll never reach your true power potential and be at constant risk for injury.

As mentioned earlier, hyper-mobility can be a negative in your swing. The reason lies in the way your muscles work. Muscles create elastic energy, but they can't store it like a rubber band does. Muscles almost immediately want to shorten and expend the energy they store while flexing, and the shorter the time delay between a stretch and shorten the more power they create. If the joints you use when you swing are hyper-mobile, the muscles around them keep on stretching (no stability), delaying the time between stretch and shorten and expending potential energy almost as quickly as it's created. At TPI, we train players who are hyper-mobile using stability exercises to help decrease the strength/shorten time delay.

NO! When your mobility is limited you can't create elastic energy and, as a result, you'll lose power potential.

NO! When you're hyper-mobile, your lack of stability makes it difficult to create torque between your mobile segments.

WARNING!
The tests on the following pages should only be attempted by healthy individuals without any pre-existing conditions. Never begin any exercise or strength-training program without first being evaluated by an expert.

POWER KEY 2: IDENTIFY YOUR POWER SOURCE

Part of the Titleist Performance Institute's power assessment plan is to measure your power sources, which are your legs, core, and arms. We measure these speed enhancers by conducting each of the tests at right utilizing a medicine ball (an 8-pound ball for men and a 4-pound ball for women and juniors). Again, the following tests should only be attempted by healthy individuals without any pre-existing conditions.

"If any of your strength or speed numbers are significantly different than the others, then it'll show up in your swing. Abusing one power source while ignoring the others typically leads to a swing fault and loss of power."

An 8-pound medicine ball can tell you a lot about why your drives are coming up short.

To see these exercises in action, visit mytpi.com for free access to hours of video lessons that show each TPI-certified test in detail. Registration is free. Type the test name in the search bar to see how it's performed.

TEST 1: Vertical Jump

Power source tested: **Leg Speed**
How to do it: Stand to the side of a wall and reach up with

1

Mark.

2

Squat.

3

Leap..

your right hand as high as possible. Mark this spot on the wall with chalk. Now, without taking a step, squat and jump as high as you can. At the apex of your leap, mark the wall with the chalk in your hand before you descend, and measure the distance between the two marks (improve your numbers with the Chair Squats and Wall Sits, next page).

How you know if it's one of your power sources:
Compare your numbers to the pros'.
LPGA Tour player:
16 - 20 inches
PGA Tour player: 18 - 22 inches
Professional long driver:
26 - 32 inches

Bring the medicine ball in...

...then let it fly.

TEST 2: Seated Chest Pass

Power source tested: **Arm Speed**

How to do it: Sit in a chair with your back straight. Bring the medicine ball into your chest with your forearms parallel to the ground. Without moving your back off the chair, push the ball straight out by extending your arms fully in front of you. Measure the longest of three attempts (improve your numbers with the Wall Bounces, next page).

How you know if it's one of your power sources: Compare your numbers to the pros'.

LPGA Tour player: 16 - 20 feet

PGA Tour player: 18 - 22 feet

Professional long driver: 26 - 32 feet

NOTE: We perform an additional test for grip strength, which is an important component for creating leverage in your swing.

TEST 3: Sit Up and Throw

Power source tested:
Core Speed and Strength

How to do it: Grab your medicine ball, lie on your back and assume a hook-line position with your knees bent at a 45-degree angle with both

feet flat on the ground as shown. Holding the medicine ball with both hands, set it above your head and then sit up and throw the ball up and forward in a smooth controlled motion. Do this three times and use your longest throw, measuring from your chest to the front of where the ball landed (improve your numbers with sit-ups and push-ups, next page).

How you know if it's one of your power sources:
Compare your numbers with the pros'.

LPGA Tour player: 16 - 20 feet

PGA Tour player: 18 - 22 feet

Professional long driver: 26 - 32 feet

IT'S YOUR TURN

The beauty of tests like the ones we perform at TPI is that they directly correlate to your individual power source(s). Ideally, all of your results should produce similar numbers; if one of your tests shows a significant difference, then this area is your weakest or strongest link.

For instance, if your leg strength is significantly more powerful than your core or push strength, you'll probably employ a vertical jump or leg-driven motion to power your swing. We see this a lot in junior players since kids develop leg strength before they develop core and upper-body strength. Watch any junior's feet and you'll see that they always spin and sometimes leave the ground as he or she tries to swing for the fences. Conversely, if you possess more upper-body strength and speed than lower-body speed and strength, you'll make your swing with mostly your arms.

The problem with placing too much emphasis on only one of your power sources is that it compromises your ability to create maximum speed. Imagine a car with eight cylinders but only six are firing. The car will still move but it won't run at maximum speed or efficiency.

The ideal scenario is one when all of your power sources are contributing equally. This makes it much easier to create smooth and efficient power. It's the reason why Tour players swing so smooth yet hit the ball so far.

Find and Exploit Your Power

Once you identify your strengths and weaknesses you can then select the in-swing moves you should experiment with to create your maximum power. In effect, you have a choice: match a swing to your body, or change your body to match the swing you want. Focus on mobility first—this gives you the ability to create torque, strength and speed. Without it you have very little chance to increase your distance off the tee. My prescription for mobility is to perform a mobility exercise one day a week for every decade you've been alive. Without it, all of the strength and power training in the world won't help you reach your power potential.

Next Steps

The exercises on the following pages show some of my favorite methods to help increase power. Each of these drills does an excellent job of building strength, speed and mobility (or stability, depending on the area) in all of your key power sources. Keep in mind, however, that in order to maximize your power sources (as well as to identify the moves you should be making in your swing to efficiently exploit them) you need to get physically screened. Take advantage of our free offer [*page 107*] and start watching the yards pile up.

Wall Sits
Good for: General body conditioning.
How to Do It: Hold a squat position with your back against the wall as shown. Don't just use your quads—pull your navel in to engage your core and focus on your glutes. Increase endurance with time.

Do 3 sets at 30 seconds each with a 30-second rest in between.

"In order to maximize your power sources you need to get physically screened."

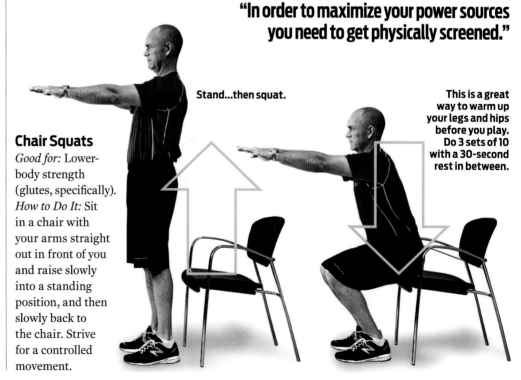

Stand...then squat.

Chair Squats
Good for: Lower-body strength (glutes, specifically).
How to Do It: Sit in a chair with your arms straight out in front of you and raise slowly into a standing position, and then slowly back to the chair. Strive for a controlled movement.

This is a great way to warm up your legs and hips before you play. Do 3 sets of 10 with a 30-second rest in between.

Basic Push-Ups

Good for: Push Strength, upper-body conditioning.
How to Do It: Perform your basic push-up, but this time go for explosive bursts and creating as much power as possible coming off the ground. Do fewer with this kind of explosiveness rather than knocking out a bunch using the regular style. Keep your elbows at your sides throughout.

Access the complete TPI exercise vault at www.mytpi.com.

Explode up...

...lower down.

Ball Chops

Good for: Core strength, improving the transition segment of your swing.
How to Do It: From a half-kneeling position, throw a medicine ball from high above your trail side downwards and across the front of your body. Slam the ball as high and as far as possible (you'll need a partner to bounce it back to you for the next rep). Keep your chest tall throughout your motion. Perform 3 sets of 10 on each side.

Kneel.

Lift.

Chop.

Watch a video of these exercises with Dave Phillips at **golf.com/bestdrivingbook.**

Trunk Rotations (Narrow Base)

Good for: Expanding range of motion.
How to Do It: Sit with your feet together and a club behind your back. Rotate your shoulders back and forth without moving your lower body. The narrow stance will challenge your stability. Don't pause between rotations and keep the club parallel to the ground. Add rotation distance and speed over time.

Rotate back and forth without moving your lower body and keeping your knees together.

Keep the shaft parallel to the ground.

Wall Bounces

Good for: Upper-body explosive speed. *How to Do It:* Throw chest passes to yourself off a wall (use a two-pound ball to start then build up). Tap all of your upper-body speed sources (chest, arms and hands). Do three sets of 10 as hard as you can—the faster the better. ●

Set up for a chest pass...

...and make rapid-fire throws and catches to build up speed.

"The ideal scenario is when all of your power sources are contributing equally."

5 THINGS TO TAKE FROM THIS CHAPTER

1 Identify your power sources and what your body is capable of doing.

2 Get physically assessed by a TPI-certified professional.

3 There are three keys to power: mobility, strength and speed.

4 You can increase power at any age if you know where to look.

5 Go play with your kids to re-learn the speed you naturally developed in your youth.

WATCH & LEARN

3-POST/HIGH-TRACK DRIVER

JAMIE SADLOWSKI

The two-time long drive champ
has the fastest swing on earth

Jamie Sadlowski proves that you don't have to be 6' 5" and able to bench press a house to hit the ball over 400 yards. At just 5' 10" and 165 pounds, Sadlowski combines a perfect blend of athleticism, strength and flexibility while rotating around not one or two posts, but three.

His setup is perfect with the club leaning back slightly to allow for the ascending blow that launches the ball high and reduces spin. His wide takeaway (with very little hip turn) creates a strong coil between his upper and lower body.

When he hinges his wrists he creates another lever for speed [*Frame 3*], and as he continues to wind his torso against his stable lower body he's ramping up energy like there's no tomorrow.

Look at the arm height [*Frame 5*]—well above Tour average. This requires great lat flexibility and shoulder range of motion. When he reaches the top he transitions with a burst of energy uncommon to most humans. You can see it in his legs (compare frame 5 to frame 6)—his lower body is starting to unwind at breakneck speed. This is the secret to massive power. Eventually, his lower body slows down so that his trunk can fire through. The lag in frame 7 is unbelievable. The rest is all about maintaining his spine angle and letting the power he stored in his backswing and wrists explode through the ball at some of the fastest speeds ever recorded.

Coil!

Lag!

KEY MOVE

Rotates around his third post (right hip) through impact and beyond.

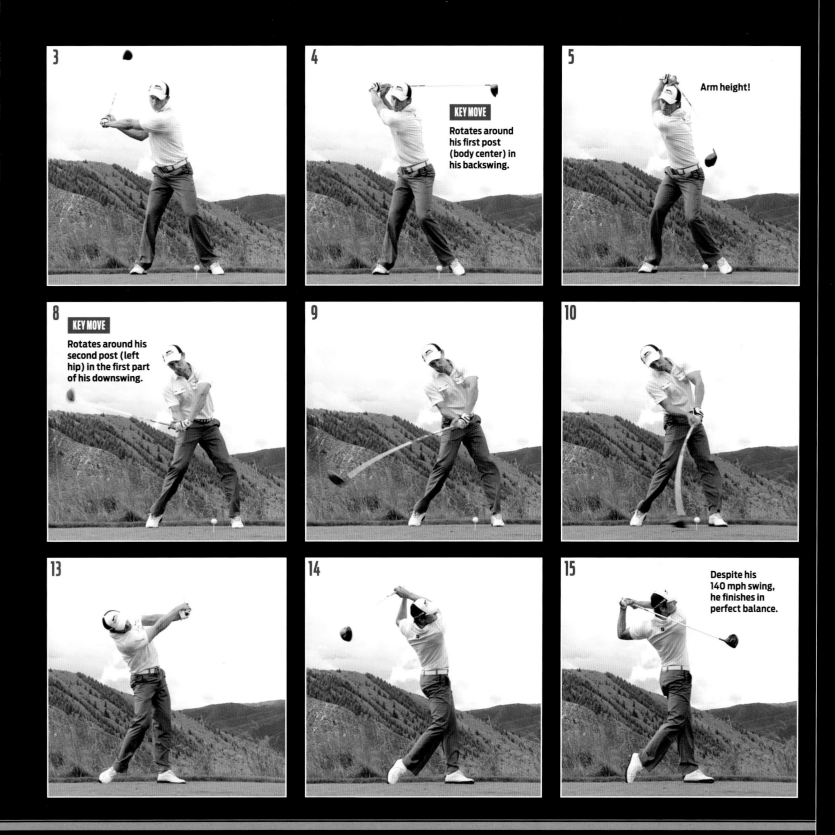

3

4

KEY MOVE

Rotates around
his first post
(body center) in
his backswing.

5

Arm height!

8

KEY MOVE

Rotates around his
second post (left
hip) in the first part
of his downswing.

9

10

13

14

15

Despite his
140 mph swing,
he finishes in
perfect balance.

CHAPTER

Research into the biodynamics of your swing shows that each segment has a desired sequence, and within that sequence there's an optimal timing aspect that allows you to create and deliver the maximum amount of energy.

BIOMECHANICS FOR A *BETTER* DRIVER SEQUENCE

Taking a segment-by-segment look at the timing and sequencing in your swing using the latest in 3D technology can help you develop a proper motion from start to finish

By **DR. ROBERT NEAL**
Golf BioDynamics
Miami, Fla.

IN BOTH GOLF AND THE EVERYDAY world people often use the terms sequencing and timing to describe the same phenomenon, but in biomechanics these two words are not interchangeable. The term sequence is used to describe the order in which events occur. For example, in the transition phase of your swing, your pelvis changes direction first, followed in order by your upper torso, arms, hands and club. Timing, on the other hand, refers to the intervals between events, and provides detailed information about the quality of the sequence. For example, if you determine the times at which each of your body segments achieves maximum speed during your downswing, you can investigate the time lags between the peaks. The important thing to keep in mind is that each phase has a desired sequence, as well as an optimal timing aspect to the sequence.

Understanding the complex motions of your body like this has been made possible only through the development of advanced 3D swing-analysis programs like the ones we use at our schools. Despite this incredible spike in technology, however, assessing the effects of sequence and timing on your overall motion remains a difficult task. To make the job a little easier, I've divided the swing into four basic phases: backswing, downswing, transition and follow-through. Most advanced analyses ignore the transition phase. I include it for the following three very important reasons.

1. There's no single point in time where every segment of your body stops moving in one direction and begins moving in the opposite direction. Thus, trying to determine a single point to denote the end of the backswing and start of the downswing is impossible.

2. Accelerating and decelerating your body segments during the transition phase organize your muscles in the optimal condition for generating force. Without this (rapid) change of direction, your body wouldn't be capable of achieving both the speed and consistency of movement that are required to swing the club properly.

3. The time following the transition (i.e., the downswing) is relatively short (250 to 300 milliseconds). Consequently, there's insufficient time to listen to any "instructions" delivered by your brain. If you want to change something about the dynamics of your impact, then it's critical that you make changes earlier in your swing.

The Charts

On the following pages you'll find a number of graphs showing pelvis, upper torso, arm, hand and club speed during different phases of your swing. When the speed is negative, it means that the body segment or club is moving to your right; when the speed is positive, then the movement is to your left. A change in sign (i.e., from positive to negative or negative to positive) of the angular velocity indicates a change of direction.

FIRST THINGS FIRST: ADDRESS

Posture at setup is one of the fundamentals that most coaches look at first when assessing a player's swing. Poor posture can lead to many problems, so it's paramount to get it right before starting the busing of assessing your motion in a biomechanical way. And since there are very few—if any—physical reasons for you to have a poor setup, there's no excuse to get it wrong. The key components to work on are as follows.

Bending

One of the most important characteristics of correct posture at setup is bending forward and establishing the relationship between your pelvis and upper torso. The ideal orientation of these body parts creates a neutral position in your back without any noticeable curves or bulges. In looking at bending posture using 3D analyses, we've pinpointed a few safety zones for each of the involved body parts. These vary a little for different age groups and from club to club.

BENDING ZONES

Pelvis: 13° - 26°
Upper torso: 27° - 40°

SET YOUR BEND
Establishing correct posture at address by bending forward using your pelvis and upper torso is Step 1 toward a biodynamically efficient swing.

UPPER TORSO BEND
Create a neutral spine (i.e., straight back) as you lean forward at address.

PELVIC BEND
You don't just lean your upper body forward—your pelvis also must tilt. Try to point your belt buckle toward the ground.

"Since there are very few—if any—physical reasons for you to have a poor setup, there's no excuse to get it wrong."

Tilting

The way you tilt at address (to the side) when hitting a driver is much different than the way you tilt when hitting one of your irons. Typically, you tilt your upper body and hips more to the right with a driver primarily because you, 1) play the ball forward in your stance, 2) you play it off a tee, and 3) your main goal is to hit up on the ball. (With an iron the goal is to create a negative angle of attack, which tilting to the right would make more difficult.)

A second reason why you tilt your spine to the right at address is because your right hand sits lower than your left on the handle. The only way to set your hands correctly on the grip while keeping your upper body parallel to the target line is to tilt your upper torso—and to some extent your pelvis—away from the target. Here are the safety zones for address tilt.

TILTING ZONES

Upper torso: 7° - 13°
Pelvis: 1° - 3°
Head: 0° - 10°

Alignment and Rotation

Alignment rule No. 1: Set your feet, knees, pelvis and upper torso so they match your intended target line. In trying to do this, most golfers make the mistake of looking at the line created between their shoulders. The error here is that your shoulders can move independently of your upper torso. If I were to ask you to "close your shoulders," you could readily do so by either pushing your left shoulder forward or pulling your right shoulder back. This change would make your shoulders look as though you're aimed to the right despite never moving your torso! Thus, to avoid ambiguity introduced by using your shoulders as points of reference, look along the line of your back—near the top of your shoulder blades—to determine where you're aimed. It's a much more reliable method.

BENDING DOS AND DON'TS

Perfect bending: Back straight and neck in line with spine.

Cocave: Arched back, head up (bifocal wearers beware).

Convex: Back rounded, head obstructing turn.

Align your body using the tops of your shoulder blades as your guides.

The fact that your right hand sits lower on the handle than your left demands that you tilt your upper body and pelvis to the right.

It's interesting to note that in the 3D world the orientation of your upper torso and pelvis are described as rotation and not alignment. Here's why: When you bend your upper body forward and tilt slightly to the right you're effectively opening up to the target, and the more you bend and tilt the more you open up. Even when you're aimed perfectly parallel left of the target line, any 3D model will read you as "rotated open." Keep an eye out for it if you ever participate in an advanced biomechanical analysis. In the meantime, simply follow these rotation safety zones:

ROTATION ZONES

Upper torso: 5° - 12° open
Pelvis: 0° - 8° open

NOTE: Our research shows that golfers who set up with their right hip higher than their left tend to sway away from the target—a bad thing—during the backswing. On the other hand, golfers who tilt their pelvis correctly (i.e., left hip higher than the right) tend to rotate rather than sway—a good thing.

BACKSWING

Your swing begins with the first movement of your body and club away from the target. Much debate surrounds how your backswing should start. Some teachers believe that you should initiate it with your arms and club while resisting their motion with your body. Instructors at the Titleist Performance Institute believe that there's an ideal takeaway sequence in which the club motions first, followed in order by your arms, upper torso and pelvis. Unfortunately, there currently isn't a consensus on the best way to begin your backswing, nor research evidence from the biomechanical literature that could support one theory over another. Regardless, we do know that once you set your swing in motion, it's critical that you load your body weight correctly as you move to the top of your backswing.

The Art of Loading Up

A frequently asked question is, "What's the number-one amateur fault?" In my opinion, failing to load and transfer weight during the swing is way up near the top of the list. Reverse-pivoting and swaying excessively away from the target during the backswing are erroneous—and damaging—movement patterns used by many golfers. If your body doesn't load correctly during your backswing, then the chances of moving in correct sequence and with good timing and speed on your downswing are substantially reduced.

Before continuing, it's prudent at this point to define a few key terms to eliminate ambiguity on the pages that follow:

Center of Mass: In mechanics, the center of mass of a rigid body is the point where you could place the entire mass of the object and it would, in a mechanical sense, behave the same. Each of your body segments has its own center of

"Once you set your swing in motion, it's critical that you load your body weight correctly as you move to the top of your backswing."

LOADING ZONE
The main goal of your backswing is to load up on your right leg without swaying and losing the spine tilts established at address.

THE TAKEAWAY SEQUENCE is best determined by closely examining the velocity of the initial movement of the club and body. In the example at right, the hands/club moved first, followed by the upper torso, the pelvis and the left arm. (The negative speed indicates that the segments are moving to the right in the backswing phase of the swing.)

> The order in which the segments begin moving is shown here. In this case, hands/club were first, upper torso second, hips third and left arm last.

> Small differences in speed and acceleration add to the confusion over the best method to start your swing. The debate continues among the instruction elite.

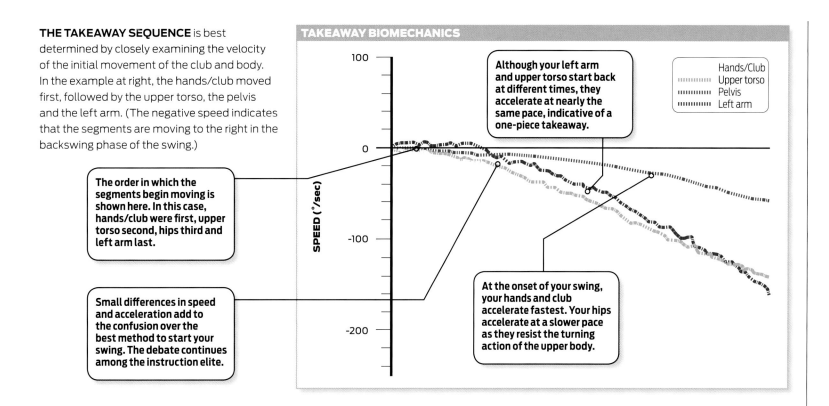

TAKEAWAY BIOMECHANICS

SPEED (°/sec)

100 / 0 / -100 / -200

Hands/Club
Upper torso
Pelvis
Left arm

> Although your left arm and upper torso start back at different times, they accelerate at nearly the same pace, indicative of a one-piece takeaway.

> At the onset of your swing, your hands and club accelerate fastest. Your hips accelerate at a slower pace as they resist the turning action of the upper body.

Keep your right hip inside your right leg—don't sway.

mass that doesn't move within the segment as the segment moves in space. Since your body is modeled as a collection of linked rigid segments, there's also a theoretical point called the **center of mass of the entire body.** This point *can* move around since it's dependent on the position and orientation of your body segments. In fact, it's even possible to have the center of mass of your entire body lie outside of your body! When biomechanists discuss weight shift (and as I'll do throughout this chapter), they're referring to the movement of the center of mass of your entire body.

Center of Pressure: Many of the new pressure platforms and force plates can pinpoint the location of your center of pressure. The center of pressure is the position on the ground where the net force is being applied. In static or quasi-static situations, the center of mass is located directly above the center of pressure. If you accelerate your center of mass, then this relationship will change due to the inertia force, but as far as center of pressure relates to your swing it's safe to assume that your center of mass and your center of pressure are always in line. Thus, force plates and pressure platforms are very useful devices to examine weight shift on the backswing (loading) and downswing (weight transfer).

In order to load correctly on your backswing, you must move your center of mass laterally, away from the target. There are numerous ways to do this and load onto your right leg. Some are more effective than others, but from a biomechanical perspective, the best way to load is to keep your pelvis relatively stable. In other words, don't sway off the ball as you rotate away from the target. Your right hip should never shift outside of your right leg, nor move toward the target, as you swing to the top. If you can avoid this error you'll create a stable platform around which your upper torso, head, arms and club can rotate away from the target. By the time you reach the top of your backswing, virtually all of these segments of your body should be farther away from the target than they were at address. If you avoid moving your pelvis toward the target, then the center of mass of your entire body will shift toward your right leg.

The longest drivers are those who shift the most weight away from the target on the backswing. Many of these players actually sway their right hip slightly away from the target (about an inch). Combined with the movement of the arms, head and upper torso away from the target, this tiny sway allows big hitters to load a greater percentage of weight onto their right leg. The percentages vary from player to player and

how you define "top of the backswing," but the majority can load as much as 85 to 90 percent of their weight on their right side at the top of the backswing. (If you choose to define the top of backswing as the point when the club changes direction like I like to do, then the load is 60 percent, which is still a significant amount at that time in the swing). Thus, if you're looking for a commonality among all great drivers, then

> **NOTE: If you're a 1-post golfer, load up on your *left* side and, stay loaded in that position throughout your motion.**

look no further than the fact that they increase the load on their right leg during the backswing. Even 1-post golfers move some weight to the right side with a driver.

The main reason for loading onto your right leg during your backswing can be readily understood

by doing a little "mind experiment." Lift your right leg off the ground so that you're balanced with all your weight on your left leg. Now, jump as high as you can by pushing down with your right foot If you can get airborne, you're superhuman! Now try to jump off your left leg—anyone can get airborne this way. The point is, in order to derive the benefit of the ground-reaction force, your feet must be in contact with the ground to begin the movement. The greater the load under your right foot at the top, the greater the frictional shear force you can apply to transfer your weight toward your left leg when you start back down to the ball. Without friction, neither weight shift nor torque applied by the ground is possible.

Stability is Key

In summary, to drive the ball with power you must first load up on your right leg, yet keep your lower body fairly stable. The increased load on your right side organizes your muscles in a state

THE BACKSWING IN MOTION

ADDRESS
Spine tilted slightly to the right.

TAKEAWAY
It starts with a turn, not a sway.

LOAD
Keep your pelvis stable so it can accept weight.

where they can generate the greatest amount of force. Further, the increased right-side load increases the maximal frictional force that's used to accelerate your center of mass toward the target during your transition. You'll have difficulty performing these key moves if you commit one or both of the following two errors:

Mistake No. 1: Moving your lower body laterally (sway) in either direction while keeping your upper torso and head "still" (i.e., no sway).
Mistake No. 2: Swaying your pelvis toward the target while either moving your upper torso and head behind the ball or keeping them still.

Committing these mistakes saps power from your downswing because you'll be unable to transfer as much weight toward your left leg on your downswing and gain the benefit of the increased momentum resulting from this shift. Keep in mind, however, that position alone is only an indicator of loading since you can't infer forces

> **"If you don't maintain your spine angle during your downswing, then it will be extremely difficult to rotate your pelvis and upper torso as fast as possible."**

based solely on how your body is oriented. In other words, looks can be deceiving (and another reason why 3D analysis has become so critical to understanding the swing in recent years).

Notes on Spine Angle
You often hear teachers and TV commentators use the phrase "maintain the spine angle" as a player is trying to increase his or her right-side load during the backswing. Spine angle is loosely defined as the angle between vertical and a line going from the center of your pelvis to the midpoint of your shoulder joints (mimicking the angle of your spine) from a side-on view. It's im-

portant to keep this angle fairly constant, neither increasing it (more forward bend) or decreasing it (spine becoming more upright). Failure to maintain a reasonably constant spine angle during your backswing leads to inconsistency. If you don't maintain your spine angle during your downswing, then it will be extremely difficult to rotate your pelvis and upper torso at max speed.

Some coaches refer to a secondary spine angle, which is the lean of your spine toward or away from the target (you set this at address as a result of your right hand being lower than your left on the grip). Maintaining this angle throughout your backswing also is crucial, and it's a good indicator that you're correctly loading onto your right leg. If you lose the angle and move your upper torso and head toward the target as you swing the club to the top, then your spine (indicated by the line between the mid-points of your hips and shoulders) will start to lean toward the target rather than maintaining its lean away from the target (like it is when you set up).

SHIFT
Big hitters get up to 90 percent of their weight on the right leg at the top.

SPINE
Keep your forward bend and your secondary tilt.

LOADED
Everything farther away from the ball than it was at address.

TRANSITION

Transition is defined as the point in time between when the first segment of your body—usually your pelvis—changes its direction of rotation, and the last segment of your body reverses its motion. The transition phase of highly skilled golfers lasts approximately 100 milliseconds (0.1 seconds). From a biomechanics perspective, the transition could easily be the most important phase of your swing since the initiation of the change of direction marks the beginning of movement toward the target.

An example may help. You're making your backswing with your hips rotating in a closed direction relative to the target line. As you approach the top of your backswing, your hips slow down and eventually come to a full stop (albeit momentarily) before they start rotating in the open direction. The instant your hips stop closing is when the transition begins. This point in time is easy to distinguish using 3D technologies. What we discovered is that in good players with sound biomechanics the pelvis is always the first segment to change direction.

Transition Sequence

The sequence good drivers employ is thus: Pelvis changes direction first, upper torso changes direction second, left arm changes direction third, and the hands an clubhead change direction last.

Recent research is now investigating the timing of the transition to gain deeper insight into the way the structures in the body are loaded and stretched prior to the downswing. It seems that an evenly spaced lag of 25 to 35 milliseconds between the changes of direction in each segment of the body is common among Tour players.

The sequence of images below and the timing graph at right show the transition-phased body positions of a very good golfer. This phase ends—and the downswing begins—once all segments have changed direction and begin moving toward the target.

The first segment of your body to change direction in a sound transition is your pelvis.

TRANSITION SEQUENCE

SLOW
As you reach the top, each body segment slows its closing rotation.

STOP
Each segment comes to a stop, but never at the same time.

START
Your pelvis should be the first to stop rotating and the first to change direction.

THE TRANSITION SEQUENCE shown in the chart at right is a biomechanical glimpse into what's probably the most important phase in your swing. The transition starts when the first segment of your body changes direction, and ends when the last segment changes direction. In sound transitions, the pelvis switches direction first (red line goes from negative to positive velocity).

The sequence of your transition is indicated by how quickly each segment crosses the line between negative (to the right) and positive (to the left) angular speed.

The sequence is clear: Pelvis first, upper torso second, arms third and your hands and club last.

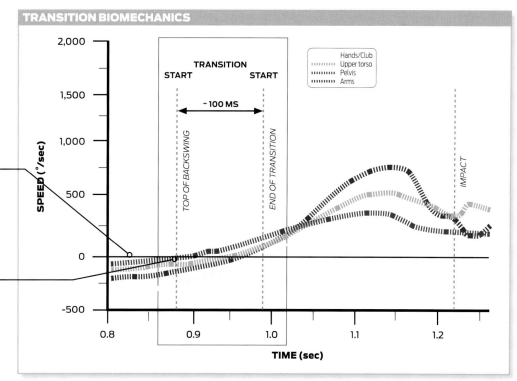

TRANSITION BIOMECHANICS

Hands/Club
Upper torso
Pelvis
Arms

TRANSITION

START — START

~ 100 MS

TOP OF BACKSWING

END OF TRANSITION

IMPACT

SPEED (°/sec)

2,000

1,500

1,000

500

0

-500

TIME (sec)

0.8   0.9   1.0   1.1   1.2

IMPORTANT
It lasts only milliseconds, but what's happening here means everything to your swing.

SEQUENCE
Hips lead, followed by shoulders, arms and finally hands and club.

END
The transition ends when all segments are closing relative to the target line.

DOWNSWING

The downswing is the most important part of your swing for transferring energy from your body to the clubhead. It begins when your hands and club finally change direction, and ends at impact. In good players, the downswing lasts around 220 to 250 milliseconds.

Weight Shift is Key

During the downswing phase of your swing you generate energy by transferring your body weight toward the target. When discussing the transition sequence, I noted that the pelvis should change direction first. This change of direction is not just a rotation of the pelvis; there must be an accompanying lateral movement toward the target. Ideally this lateral move should initiate your forward weight shift at the start of your downswing, and you need to do it without moving your upper torso and head. Of course, the

Don't stop your body at impact—brace it.

extent of this lateral shift depends on whether you're a rotary or lateral golfer [*see Chapter 3*].

As you move more and more weight toward your left lead leg as you get closer to impact, you should feel an increase in speed and energy in

your body. Eventually, the lateral momentum that you've built up must be reduced, or "stabilized," for impact. Don't confuse this with "stop." Brace your left leg while at the same time allowing your upper body to rotate. Here's a checklist for your impact position:

> **Pelvic tilt:** 10° - 12° (left hip higher)
> **Pelvic rotation:** 35° - 55° open
> **Pelvic rise:** 0.5" - 1.0"
> **Head drop:** 2.0" - 3.0"

Your left arm should be fully extended and with your hands higher than they were at address. The increase in hand height is due to the inertia of the clubhead. A good analogy of the phenomenon is when you spin a small rock or weight on the end of a string. As you spin the object it begins to lift up, and the faster you rotate it, the more it rises (until it's level with your hand). This is something I don't recommend you think about doing, but it nonetheless is a very real scenario in a solid impact position.

DOWNSWING SEQUENCE

START
Pelvis turns first paired with a lateral shift.

PELVIS
Reaches top speed then slows down.

SHOULDERS
Pick up the speed, max out, then slow down.

THE DOWNSWING SEQUENCE graph at right illustrates the motions of a professional golfer. The downswing begins when the last segment in the body-segment chain changes direction (i.e., the velocity changes from negative to positive), and ends at impact.

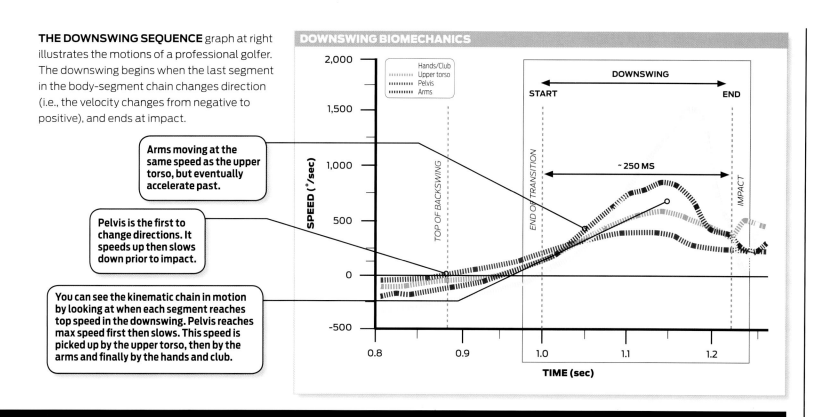

DOWNSWING BIOMECHANICS

Legend:
- Hands/Club
- Upper torso
- Pelvis
- Arms

DOWNSWING
START — END

~ 250 MS

TOP OF BACKSWING

END OF TRANSITION

IMPACT

SPEED (°/sec): 2,000 / 1,500 / 1,000 / 500 / 0 / -500

TIME (sec): 0.8 / 0.9 / 1.0 / 1.1 / 1.2

Arms moving at the same speed as the upper torso, but eventually accelerate past.

Pelvis is the first to change directions. It speeds up then slows down prior to impact.

You can see the kinematic chain in motion by looking at when each segment reaches top speed in the downswing. Pelvis reaches max speed first then slows. This speed is picked up by the upper torso, then by the arms and finally by the hands and club.

ARMS
Pick up the speed, max out, then slow down.

HANDS/CLUB
Pick up the speed transferred by the decrease in arm speed.

IMPACT
Stabilizing and bracing your body allow the clubhead to whip through the ball.

Body Segment Relationships

One of the oldest pieces of advice in golf is to "keep your head down." While this advice would be good for someone whose head is moving all over the place, it's not true of great drivers of the ball. Your head is attached to your body and, as a result, needs to move with it—a little behind the ball on your backswing, and a bit toward the target on your downswing. Also, you need to rotate your head along with your upper torso turn to minimize the stresses on your neck. A good thought is to "follow the ball with your head." In other words, rotate your head to track the ball's flight once you make contact.

The last comment I'll make is about your spine and the importance of maintaining its angle—it's good to do for your swing and for your body. It's not always easy to do, however. Your arms and club build up a ton of inertia as they come down into impact, a force that tends to pull your upper body toward the ball. If you lack sufficient muscular strength in your back to resist this pull, then the ligaments of your spine will take up

Maintaining your spine angle is key for power and preventing injury.

the load. One of the undesired side-effects with this load-sharing situation is that it increases the compressive stress on the discs of the spine. Over time and with many repetitions the load could lead to damage to your intervertebral discs!

FOLLOW-THROUGH

Your follow-through is all about absorbing the kinetic energy you generated during your downswing, but failed to transfer to the ball. Although what your body or club do after impact has no influence on trajectory, it can help you prevent injury. A good piece of advice is to allow your swing to trace a smooth, long arc up to your finish. There's no need to rush after the ball's already on it's way. Plus, having a reasonably large distance over which to release the kinetic energy in your body means it doesn't have to work as hard than if the follow-through was short. Basically, your body has less chance of sustaining injury with a long follow-through than a short one.

The key is that you can learn a lot about and improve your swing with biodynamics. Have your swing checked using the latest 3D technology—you'll see your swing in a whole new light. ●

FOLLOW-THROUGH SEQUENCE

IMPACT
Energy transferred to ball.

ANGLE
If your back isn't up to snuff, you'll lift up through the ball—not good.

FOLLOW-THROUGH
Body absorbs energy that failed to transfer.

FINISH
Use a longer forward-swing to keep injury at bay.

COPY THIS!
The acceleration-deceleration profile of the key body segments at right is the hallmark of good kinematics. Key is that the last segment in the chain, the clubhead [*light blue line*], reaches peak speed close to impact. The correct timing during the downswing is one of the most important characteristics that determines the efficiency of your body movements are. The data from the best ball strikers in the world show timing lags between the peak speeds of approximately 30 milliseconds. Also notice how the lines are very smooth, indicating that the body parts are passing energy from one segment to the next.

NOT THIS!
Here, the accelerations and decelerations indicate a lack of stability and body-segment control of a less-than-accomplished golfer. The graph shows incorrect timing of peak speeds in the downswing. In particular, you can see that the arm segment reaches its peak before any of the other segments. and there's a "double peak" of the upper torso's rotational velocity.

Data taken from pro and amateur swings with a 6-iron; differences are more severe with a driver.

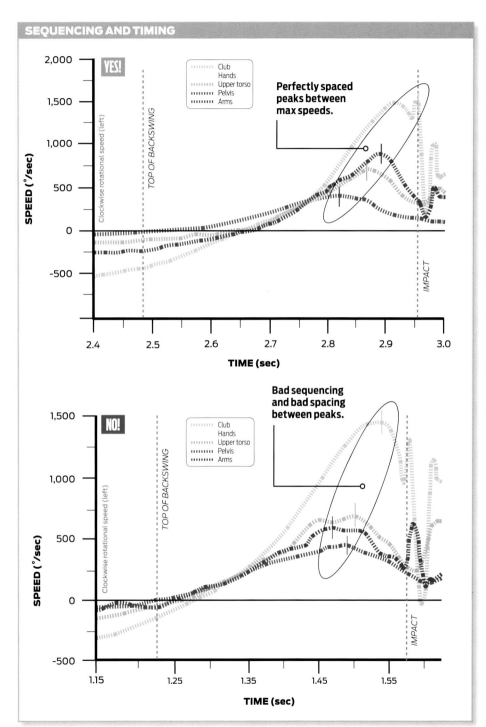

5 THINGS TO TAKE FROM THIS CHAPTER

1 3D technology and biomechanics are changing the way instructors and players look at the swing.

2 The technology is so powerful it tracks what each segment of your body is doing at every millisecond of your motion.

3 The acceleration/deceleration profiles of your body segments in the transition and downswing grade you as either biomechanically efficient or inefficient.

4 The best way to fix inefficiencies during your downswing and impact is to make changes to the phases of your swing that precede them.

5 Better address and backswing technique allow for a better downswing kinematic sequence— the secret to hitting the ball farther and more accurately.

Special thanks to instruction model Paul Park.

1-POST/MID-TRACK DRIVER
ZACH JOHNSON

The former Masters champ is a
1-post model of driving consistency

It's often said that a consistent swing is the key to great golf, and there's no better example than 2007 Masters champion Zach Johnson. While Zach may be best known for his steady putter and hard work around the greens, he's no slouch off the tee, either. The secret to his success is simple: symmetry. Symmetry equals repeatability, and repeatability equals consistency.

Notice how Zach anchors his weight over his left leg (the hallmark setup trait of a 1-post golfer), and also how he flares out his left foot to enhance his rotation around his front post [Frame 4]. Initially, he works the club out but then up via his wrist hinge. This is a great checkpoint for mid-track players: When your hands are at waist height, the shaft should bisect your right forearm.

Following the lead of his arms and hands, Zach's shoulders and hips begin to do their job of turning away from the target. His left shoulder works under his chin and his right hip turns behind him [Frame 5].

When he reaches the top he flexes his left knee [Frame 6]. This allows him to stay anchored over his front post. He then clears his left hip and his trunk so that the club can slot down to his right-arm plane [Frame 8] and deliver the club to the ball on his best path. Notice how he never stops rotating over his front leg until his swing is finished.

1

KEY MOVE
Establishes his front anchor at address and flares his left foot.

2

6

KEY MOVE
He flexes his left knee to maintain his front-leg post.

7

11

12

KEY MOVE
He never stops turning around his front-leg post.

3

4 Sets the club with a solid wrist hinge.

5

8 Hips and torso clear to re-track the club on his right-arm plane.

9

10

13

14

15

CHAPTER

Your flexibility decreases over time. Buck the trend while also offsetting the effects of posture decline to keep your drives moving down the fairway at any age.

GET THE *MOST* FROM YOUR
RANGE OF MOTION

Every golfer is beset by structural and physical limitations. Here's how to adjust for them to produce quality drives with the swing you have now, and eventually eliminate them for good.

By **JON TATTERSALL, PGA** *&* **BRIAN YEE, P.T.**
Terminus Club Atlanta, Ga.

THE PROBLEM WITH GOLF IS THAT the people who play it get older. Everyone loses strength and flexibility over time—sometimes too fast. You work too hard, you sleep too little and although you may hit the gym or jog from time to time, there's no doubt that you're not the athlete—or even the human being—you were twenty, 10 or even 5 years ago, and it's having a serious and negative effect on your game.

The fact that it's getting more and more difficult for you to tie your shoes in the morning, or that you catch yourself slouching more and more when you see your reflection in a mirror, or that you can't muster the energy to hit through a bucket of balls or practice your putting for more than 20 minutes at a time, should tell you a lot about why you're not driving the ball as far as you once did. The structural and postural toll Father Time takes on your game is very real, and likely the main reason why you've seen your index steadily climb and your driving distance decrease to the point where now even the white tees pose a severe test. Even if you're a young golfer there are ways your body can creep up on you to limit what you can do with a club in your hands. Young people lose flexibility and range of motion just as easily as older players if they fail to lead an athletic lifestyle or dedicate enough time to maintaining the most important piece of equipment you own—your body.

Our goal at Terminus Club in Atlanta—a high-tech golf training center staffed by a specially trained team of instruction professionals, physical therapists, strength and conditioning experts and biomechanics personnel—is to make your body move as efficiently as possible as it relates to your swing, and increase what Tour pros have and amateurs don't: strength through range of motion. The best thing about our approach is that the benefits it lends to your driver swing carry over to everything else that you do—the possibility of better golf becomes a catalyst to improve your physical fitness and get back into the game of life.

Our plan of attack with each student is two-fold: 1) To get you in position to limit the negative effect of your structural and muscular limitations so you can drive the ball farther and score better with the body you have right now, and 2) Work out the kinks in every conceivable way to take years off your game and strokes off your card, while adding power and speed you haven't seen in ages.

Golf is a game that's meant to be played for a lifetime. Don't let the slow breakdown of your physical strengths and abilities (as well as your range of motion) stop the game from being the fun, enjoyable and rewarding experience it is. Test what your body can do and apply the quick fixes and long-term repairs presented on these pages, as well as the key adjustments to your setup and swing as presented by posture expert Roger Fredericks later in this chapter [see page 150], and you'll be turning more than a few heads off the tee, regardless of your age, ability and commitment to fitness.

PART 1:
RANGE OF MOTION LIMITATIONS

There's one major thing pros have over amateurs: greater range of motion.

My business partner, Todd Townes, and I have been studying golfers' strength and range of motion parameters—and the effects they have on their swings—for the better part of 13 years. It's been a journey into functional movement and swing technique deeper than we ever thought possible. During this time we've collected thousands of hours of 3D-motion analyses, which we've studied with biomechanics experts, performance coaches and physical therapists. To further examine our students' abilities and our collective theories, we've invested a few hundred thousand dollars into technology to measure movement for a variety of sports. Basically, we're into your body's role in helping you hit the ball farther and play better.

Our process typically begins with physically testing the player, regardless of their ability. We put them through balance, range-of-motion and strength tests as they relate to the swing, then measure their motion with a club in their hands on one of our two 3D-motion systems.

We balance the information we gain during this testing to determine appropriate courses of action. Almost every student starts with a flexibility wellness program. Once they achieve a certain level of motion, the strength team takes over. All the while we implement swing changes and moves based on the development of the student until all cylinders are firing and the player is once again driving the ball with max efficiency.

Our ultimate goal is for every golfer in search of peak performance to seek out a program like ours to get the most from your driving body.

However, we understand that's not often feasible. Time, money, family, work and an inability to agree to a long-term commitment make it difficult for most players to accelerate through such a program. No hard feelings. We only hope that you one day make an effort to do so—it'll pay off in serious yards and lower scores. In the meantime, we'll provide you with a group of self-tests in this chapter that you can perform in the comfort of your own living room to assess your golf body, and then show you how to apply this information to help you improve the swing you have right now and, as you make changes to your body's range of motion, increase your balance, flexibility and driving strength for the future.

What to Expect

As much as you need to develop additional power and strength to hit the ball farther, proper flexibility and range of motion in specific joints is critical for you to produce proper force generation and, more important, the most efficient mechanics to prevent injuries. Hence the tests—each is specifically designed to determine your mobility in key anatomical areas [*see list, below*]. Depending on how you do, you'll either consult our in-swing and setup adjustments to make the most of a limited range of motion right now, or seek the strength and stretching exercises to get rid of them for good.

The Tests
1. Hip/leg range of motion (left and right)
2. Neck range of motion
3. Lat range of motion
4. Trunk rotation
5. Right shoulder motion (external)
6. Left shoulder range of motion (internal)

Hip/Leg Range of Motion

Your left leg (whether you're a 1- or 2-post golfer) is your primary swivel point in your downswing. It's also a major stability area, and you generate the greatest amount of horsepower when you shift and rotate onto it during the downswing and follow-through segments of your motion. The problem is that you need sufficient range of motion in this area to shift and rotate correctly.

Using your left leg as both a swivel and stability point also helps you balance. Balance is a generic term thrown around all-too liberally by teachers and players alike. Most golfers think that merely saying the word "balance" is all that's needed to make it happen. If you fail the left hip internal rotation tests on the next page, then balance will be an issue for you. This is a bad thing because finishing in a balanced position and shifting from your right leg to your left leg during your downswing is a major part of the power production and delivery systems in your swing.

Your right leg, on the other hand, functions more as a cocking lever, absorbing energy created in your backswing for your body to use when it shifts left (much like your right arm cocking when you rear back to throw a baseball). It, too, requires a substantial range of motion for your swing to reach its maximum power potential.

Your right leg and hip act like a cocking lever in your swing.

Your left leg and hip function as both pivot and stability points.

"If you fail the internal rotation tests on the next page, then balance will be an issue for you."

TAKE THE TEST: LEFT HIP INTERNAL ROTATION

WHAT IT DOES: Measures the flexibility in your left leg and hip. The more flexible you are in these areas, the harder you can shift onto and pivot around your left side during your downswing.

HOW TO TAKE IT: Lay face down with your knees inches apart. Bend your left leg 90 degrees so that the sole of your shoe is pointing straight up. Slowly lower your left heel to your left side, keeping your knee bent at 90 degrees and your pelvis and waist stationary. Stop when you can't lower your left heel any further without discomfort, then measure the distance that your heel moved from its vertical starting point.

TEST PASSED: If you can lower your left heel in the pass zone [*photo, below*], then you have ample flexibility and range of motion in your left leg and hip.

TEST FAILED: If your left leg stops in the fail zone pictured below then you have limited flexibility and range of motion in your left leg and hip. Balance will be an issue for you. Further studies indicate a prevalence of lower back pain in golfers with less than 27 degrees of internal rotation in their left leg.

WARNING: If your left heel moves beyond the pass zone, you have too much mobility, which is as damaging a liability as too little.

Limited hip range of motion won't allow you to separate your upper body from your lower, so go ahead and turn everything together while focusing on setting the club on your natural track.

START

FAIL

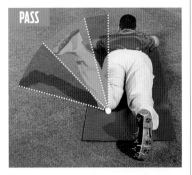
PASS

HYPER-MOBILE

Test Your Right Hip

Perform the test again with your right leg, recording the distance your right heel travels (in degrees) from its starting position. It's critical that your right leg have adequate internal rotation. Without it (approximately 45 degrees using this test), your knees, trunk or shoulders will be forced to compensate, costing you precious energy.

The less internal range of motion you have in your right hip, the less potential energy it will be able to absorb when you load up during your backswing.

If You Failed the Test

Limited hip mobility won't allow you to correctly pivot onto your right leg in your backswing. Instead, you'll move beyond it, swaying too far off the ball with very little chance to get back to your left side on your way back down. There's also a high probability that you won't be able to separate your upper body from your lower and build sufficient coil like you should.

Unfortunately, you can't make a "model" swing with a poor hip range of motion. The good news is that you can make a "functional" one. A way around the

Since limited hip mobility sets you up to sway past your right side, pivot around your left.

problem is to forget about resisting with your lower body and turn everything together [*photo, above left*]. You'll lose energy, but at least you'll have a better shot at keeping your club on plane than you do with swaying. The second option is to avoid pivoting onto your right hip all together (your hip won't allow it anyway) and simply rotate around your left hip (1-post style) from start to finish [*above*].

Regardless of which adjustment you go for, it's important that you go for at least one. Swaying off the ball is bad news in any swing.

Easy Adjustments

If you tested for hip tightness, try flaring out both feet at address, somewhere in the 30- to 45-degree range [*top photo, below*]. Flaring will give you more hip flexibility compared to when your feet are square (so can dropping your right foot back).

If you tested for hyper-mobility (more typical in juniors and women than in men), do the opposite—set both feet square to your line to restrict your hips' range of motion (or square the one on the same side as the hip that tested for hyper-mobility in the event of a mismatch).

Another good way to overcome a hyper-mobility problem is to bow your knees out at address, setting them directly over your ankles [*bottom left*]. Then, on your downswing, try to get your left hip over your left knee to brace your hips through impact [*bottom right*]. This move slows your forward movement so the next part of your kinetic chain can pick up the speed.

Flaring your feet at address can make inflexible hips a bit more mobile [*left*]. Also try dropping your right foot back.

Squaring your stance [*below left*] and creating a brace at impact [*right*] are ways to reel in hips with too much range of motion.

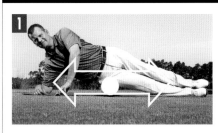

Roll It Out

Place a foam roller under your hip and roll over it back and forth, massaging the hip fascia and breaking up restrictions.

Stretch It Out

Lay on your back and simultaneously pull your knee and ankle toward your torso for a good hip stretch. Do it on both sides.

Work It Out

With an elastic band attached to your left ankle, pull your left leg sideways (working your lateral hip muscles). Perform several reps then repeat with other leg.

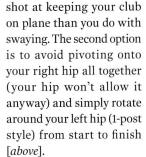

Neck Range of Motion

Your neck is more important to your swing than you realize. It's actually one of three pieces that make up your spine, and if it's suffering from any lack in range of motion, then you're going to have severe difficulties turning your chest under your chin like you should. The reason why is that if your chin can't move in relation to your chest, then how can you expect your chest to move in relation to your chin? This is why the classic tip, "keep your head still," is bad medicine for most people. The majority of players need more neck mobility than less.

"If your chin can't move in relation to your chest, then how can you expect your chest to move in relation to your chin?"

Learn more about these range of motion flaws and fixes at
golf.com/bestdrivingbook

TAKE THE TEST: Cervical Mobility

WHAT IT DOES: Gauges the mobility of your neck.

HOW TO TAKE IT: The test for neck mobility is to sit on a Swiss ball or chair, fold your arms across your chest and simply turn your head to the right and left. Keep your ears in line with your shoulders and don't allow your chest to turn along with your head.

TEST PASSED: If you can get your chin to point at your shoulder in either direction, then you have ample neck range of motion.

TEST FAILED: If you can't point your chin at your shoulder in either direction, then you have limited neck range of motion.

PASS

FAIL

Everyday tasks like using the phone, working at a desk and even flying on a plane can cause your neck mobility to decrease. An easy check is to look at your profile in a mirror—if your ears are in front of your shoulders then you probably have neck mobility issues.

Poor neck mobility forces you to move your head and sway as you turn.

That's okay—just make an equal sway forward as you turn through the ball.

HOW TO FIX IT FOR GOOD

Stretch It Out

Sit on a Swiss ball (ideally, but a chair works) and gently pull your head down and in line with your shoulders. Hold for 20 seconds, then work the other side. It's better to do 5 reps each day than 20 reps every so often. Also, keep taking the test above.

If You Failed the Test

A sufficient level of cervical mobility allows you to keep your head in place as you turn your left shoulder under your chin in your backswing. If you lack sufficient mobility, your head will move as you rotate your shoulders, resulting in a significant sway off the ball [*photo, above left*]. Golfers who aren't aware that they have a neck mobility problem usually aren't aware that they sway, either, so if you failed the test, make sure you sway back on your downswing. Try to get your entire body moving toward the target as you turn through the ball [*above right*]. It's a controversial idea and hardly ideal, but a forward sway will help until you fix your neck mobility for good.

Lat Range of Motion

"The best players in the world are much better at pulling objects than pushing them."

From studying some of the best players in the world we know that they have stronger posterior muscles (those in the back) than anterior muscles (those in the front), and that they're much better at pulling objects than pushing them. You're probably just the opposite, in part due to the exercises you prefer to do at the gym (i.e., bench press), and as a result are underdeveloped and tight in your posterior muscles, including those in your lats. This presents a problem because lats are part of your overall shoulder structure, and therefore are needed to rotate your body, work your arms up and down and swing the club on your preferred plane, whether it's low, middle or high.

TAKE THE TEST: Lat Mobility

WHAT IT DOES: Tests the flexibility in your lats. The more flexible you are here, the more likely you are to get the club on your preferred plane in your backswing.

HOW TO TAKE IT: Stand erect with your hands at your sides, then raise both arms up as far as they can go above your head, like you're a NFL umpire signaling a touchdown.

TEST PASSED: Healthy lat range of motion should allow you to raise both arms overhead at least 90 degrees from horizontal [*photo*].

TEST FAILED: You cant raise your arms past your head, or are able to pass the test with only one of your arms. You want both arms to reach the same place overhead, otherwise it's a failed test.

YOU CHEATED: Tilting backward to get both arms high above your head is not allowed (notice in the "cheat" photo how my arms are straight up but still ahead of the center line). Keep your head and spine in line when you do take this test.

If You Failed the Test

Notice that with good lat mobility [*photo, below left*] everything is moving as it should and I'm able to swing my arms—and club—exactly where I want to. With poor lat flexibility [below right] my arms have swung higher relative to my chest turn and I've lost their connection with my torso (a bad thing if you tested out as a 1-planer in Chapter 3). Basically, if your lats are compromised, you'll be an up-and-down swinger whether you want to be or not.

Swing back low and short if lat inflexibility is causing your arms to raise in your backswing.

YES
Functional lats allow you to move the club wherever you want it to go.

NO
Poor lat mobility forces you to lift your arms and lose connection with your chest.

Easy Adjustments

Counter lat inflexibility by swinging your arms lower. You'll have to pair this low-arm motion with a shorter backswing. While this isn't ideal it's better than allowing your arms to lift up. Dana Quigley and Dan Pohl played on the PGA Tour with backswings not much longer than what I'm showing here.

HOW TO FIX IT FOR GOOD

Stretch It Out

While seated, raise your driver over your head as shown, making sure that your hands, shoulders and hips are lined up and your lower body is stable. Lean right, creating a gentle stretch through the side of your body. Repeat with the left side.

If you can't get your hands above your head, then simply perform the test on the opposite page. It's as much an exercise as it is a way to test your mobility.

Trunk Rotation

Most golfers know that rotating their trunk is key to making a solid swing. What we focus on at Terminus Club is not only the quantity of your trunk motion, but more important, the quality of the motion.

Quantity: Elite golfers (professional and collegiate), can rotate their spines in the range of 80 to 110 degrees during the backswing and follow-through. Younger golfers also have the flexibility in their spines to rotate this much in most cases. Since the human spine stiffens with age, older golfers tend to rotate less.

Quality: Your spine is comprised of three major parts: cervical area (neck), thoracic area (middle back/rib cage), and lumber area (lower back). Biomechanics and anatomical studies show that your trunk rotates predominately from the thoracic area of the spine, with secondary contributions from the lumbar region. It's often the case that a student can adequately rotate his or her trunk, but do it in a way that's biomechanically inefficient. In a perfect scenario your spine rotates smoothly using evenly distributed motion from vertebra to vertebra, with your middle back dominating the action. That doesn't mean it can't—or won't—break from ideal and rotate from an isolated area of the spine, which typically happens with a loss of range of motion.

People argue that as long as they have the available range of motion that's needed to swing then it doesn't matter how it's done. From an injury-prevention and force-production standpoint, it's a weak debate. Rotating your spine from the right area and utilizing an even distribution of vertebra is critical for optimal and efficient trunk rotation.

What we find is that many golfers are so limited in their trunk range of motion that they end of rotating predominately from one or two vertebrae to compensate for their lack of mobility,

"In a perfect scenario your spine rotates smoothly using evenly distributed motion from vertebra to vertebra, with your middle back dominating the action."

then complain of pain in those areas. Depending on posture and other related mechanics, most golfers experience pain in either the lower back or mid-back for this reason. If this is starting to sound familiar, then it's likely you can trace your back pain problems to your spine failing to rotate in an efficient manner when you swing.

Another thing to consider is that most of your abdominal muscles attach to your rib cage. Your abs are the primary force producers in your trunk. The key is that your ribs start from the thoracic spine, and if your thoracic spine isn't rotating properly then your abdominal muscles won't be in the proper biomechanical position to provide the most effective contraction and force production.

TAKE THE TEST: Trunk Rotation

WHAT IT DOES: Tests the quality and quantity of your turning ability.

HOW TO DO IT: Sit on a Swiss ball and cross your arms over your chest, then simply rotate left and right. Measure your turn from the middle of your sternum in your starting position to the middle of your sternum where you can no longer rotate comfortably. (Perform this test in your address posture to see if there's a difference). Also, have a friend watch you from the back to check for smooth curvature in your spine when rotating both ways. Often, players rotate smoothly in one direction and not so smoothly in the other (i.e., uneven or localized rotation). To really assess your curvature, perform the test with your shirt off.

TEST PASSED: You're able to rotate your sternum at least 60 degrees.

TEST FAILED: You're unable to rotate your sternum at least 60 degrees. Repeating this test frequently might give you the numbers you desire since this is an exercise as well as a test.

like they see the pros do on TV. They may get to parallel, but they'll do it with a loss of arc and almost zero chance of approaching the ball on the correct angle. If you're the type of player who hits his short irons longer than normal but can't get off the tee box, this could be your problem.

If you tested out for limited trunk motion, either in quality or quantity, fight the urge to over-swing or overuse your arms and instead make your backswing shorter. Approach every shot like you're hitting it with a three-quarter swing, including your tee shots.

Easy Adjustments

In addition to shortening up your backswing, add more lower-body lateral motion to balance out the steep arc that comes with over-swinging so you can create a shallower angle of attack. To do this, push hard off your right leg and onto your left leg at the beginning of your downswing. It will take a bit of strength and flexibility in your lower body to make it happen, so if your body isn't up to the task then plan for a predominately pull/fade shot pattern. Forget about trying to hit a draw because you don't have anything in your body motion to shallow out your swing.

HOW TO FIX IT FOR GOOD

Roll It Out

Rolling your mid-back over a foam roll will help improve your thoracic mobility. If quality is your problem and you're in pain, seek the advice of a qualified physical therapist who can improve your spine mechanics.

If You Failed the Test

When your ability to rotate from your thoracic spine (middle back) is compromised, it's very likely that you'll overuse your arms to get what you feel is a long enough backswing. Once your arms swing past your shoulder's most comfortable range of motion, however, they'll lift. What you're left with is a too-steep backswing that's far too long and in position to create a too-narrow downswing arc. Don't expect to win any long-drive prizes at your next outing from this type of swing.

Instead of overusing the arms some golfers with limited trunk rotation make up for it by bending their left elbow, again with a desire to swing the club all the way back until it's parallel

Right Shoulder Range of Motion

Shoulder rotation is vital to making an effective swing, and you need two types: external and internal. External rotation has more to do with the role of your right shoulder as you motion the club to the top of your backswing. The best way to think about external rotation in your right shoulder is to picture the cocking motion of a pitcher's throwing arm. To get a *feel* for it, hold your upper arm at a horizontal angle with your forearm pointing straight up and then slowly cock your right hand back [*see test, opposite page*]. If your right shoulder external rotation is compromised, then you're going to have a difficult time setting the club on plane and controlling the clubface. The situation is exacerbated by the presence of limited external rotation in your left shoulder. Limited external shoulder rotation is common in both arms since most of us spend our days in front of a computer with our arms and hands in front of us, not behind us. The problem, like with any of the ranges of motion discussed in this chapter, is that an imbalance between your left and right sides will invariably lead to compensations.

"If your right shoulder external rotation is compromised, then you're going to have a difficult time setting the club on plane and controlling the clubface."

TAKE THE TEST: External Shoulder Rotation

WHAT IT DOES: Tests your right shoulder external range of motion, which is needed to swing your club back on plane and to eliminate the possibility of unduly opening the clubface. The professional golfers we've tested average about 110 degrees of external shoulder rotation (measured from a horizontal starting position).

HOW TO TAKE IT: Push your right arm straight out to the side from your right shoulder and bend your right elbow 90 degrees, keeping your elbow in line with your shoulder. Without disturbing this arrangement, slowly cock your right upper arm back [*photo, below left*].

TEST PASSED: You hit the pass zone shown below and are able to bend your arm past your right ear.

TEST FAILED: You can't even bend your arm *to* your ear let alone past it.

YOU CHEATED: You need to tilt back to hit the pass zone.

Easy Adjustments

Don't push the end range of your right shoulder range of motion. Instead, focus more on getting your clubface, left wrist and left forearm to line up. Keeping your right elbow in tight helps, as does making a more compact backswing. Don't sacrifice clubface position for extra backswing length.

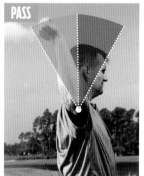

If You Failed the Test

Expect to see your right elbow fly if you swing beyond your right shoulder external range of motion. The higher your right elbow, the more your left wrist will cup, opening the clubface. Hello, slice.

Another Way to Test Your Rotation

The exercise above where you test your right shoulder external rotation with your arm at horizontal is an excellent way to gauge your overall right shoulder range of motion. However, it really only tells you half the story. It's just as important to measure the external range of motion in your right shoulder with your elbow directly at your side [*photos, below*]. This second method allows you to determine if your limited range of motion is due to muscle tightness (easy to fix) or a joint limitation (a larger concern). A lot of the golfers we test with shoulder pain can pass the test above, but not the one at left since it deals more with the quality of your rotation and not quantity. It's important that you perform both tests.

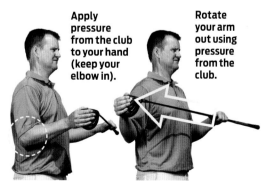

Apply pressure from the club to your hand (keep your elbow in).

Rotate your arm out using pressure from the club.

Re-take the Second Test

Use the secondary test at left as an exercise to improve the overall external rotation of your shoulders. After applying pressure and rotating your arm outward, hold for 10 to 15 seconds (do 10 to 15 reps). At no point should you feel pain. Keep a log to track any improvement.

Left Shoulder Range of Motion

You need ample left shoulder range of motion in your backswing and, specifically, internal flexibility in order to make sure your left arm swings across your body and not up. If you're limited here you'll probably track the club higher than you want. Internal range of motion also is important in your right arm, but in a different segment of your motion. As you swing down and past impact your right arm should work across your body, which is difficult to do with limited internal rotation. Although internal rotation is more associated with left shoulder action in your swing, symmetry is always important. Favoring one side of your body over the other will typically show up in your motion as a swing flaw.

If You Failed the Test

Limited internal rotation in your left shoulder affects your swing in much the same way as limited lat range of motion [*page 142*], causing you to lift up your arms in your backswing and lose the important connection between your left arm and your chest. Keep in mind that poor right shoulder rotation also affects how your left arm operates since you hold the club with both hands. To swing back and through properly you need a blend of quality internal and external rotation in both shoulders.

TAKE THE TEST: Internal Shoulder Rotation

WHAT IT DOES: Tests the internal flexibility in your left shoulder.
HOW TO DO IT: Set your forearm and bicep perpendicular to the ground and out in front of you as shown, then push down gently on the back of your left hand with your right.

TEST PASSED: You can get your left arm to bend at least 40 degrees.
TEST FAILED: You can't get your left arm to bend at least 40 degrees.
YOU CHEATED: You're able to bend your arm at least 40 degrees, but you lifted your left elbow to do it.

STEP 1

Swing your left arm across your body and set your right hand behind your left elbow...

START

PASS

CHEAT

Easy Adjustments

Left shoulder internal rotation is a big-time problem even with athletic golfers since most people favor pushing exercises in the gym and, therefore, have fuller chests. The best thing you do is swing your left arm across your body in a mock backswing, then slowly pull it in close to your chest using your right hand [*photos, below*]. You should feel a gentle warming across the top of your left shoulder if you do it correctly (keep your left arm straight). This is a very effective and simple pre-round warm-up.

STEP 2

...then pull your left arm in to your chest as much as you can. This is the left shoulder internal rotation you're looking for.

HOW TO FIX IT FOR GOOD

Stretch It Out

Enhance your internal rotation stretch by lying on your side as shown and applying gentle downward pressure to your hand while keeping your elbow on the ground. Remember to work both shoulders.

Arm Lifts

Lay on your stomach with your hands placed on the ground by your ears. Slowing lift one forearm off the ground keeping your elbow down and without raising the shoulder to your ear. This helps stabilize the rotational strength of your shoulder.

Work It Out

Using the cable-pull machine at your gym, gently pull back the cables while "pinching" your shoulder blades together (don't elevate your shoulders—keep them level). Strengthening your shoulder blade muscles like this can help improve their overall stability when you swing.

Adding Power

Taking the tests, making the necessary adjustments in your setup and swing and using the stretches on these pages to increase your range of motion in key areas of your anatomy will give you the flexibility—and swing—you had in your prime. The next step: adding power.

Most golfers confuse "adding power" with "getting stronger," then wonder why all that extra gym time never pays off. At Terminus Club we have a philosophy to explain how you should best approach developing your body. **Key to this philosophy is that you can't increase strength without the flexibility to handle it, and vice versa. The goal is to develop your body with an eye toward balance,** between both your flexibility and strength in the front of your body and the back. If you feel like your body is flexible enough to handle some additional power, follow our exercises on **golf.com/bestdrivingbook**.

PART 2:
POSTURAL LIMITATIONS

By **ROGER FREDERICKS**, PGA
Fredericks Golf, Carlsbad, Calif.

Despite our varied individual body types, the truth is that there's really only one type of posture that allows you to function and perform optimally. In this ideal and fundamentally correct posture, the joints in your body all line up, with your shoulder joints over your hips, your hips over your knees, and your knees over your ankles. This is what I call a **Four Socket Position**, and it's the best arrangement for athletic movement. When your posture matches the Four Socket Position you can swing with the proper kinesthetic sequence starting from the ground up and deliver maximum power to the ball.

FUNCTIONAL POSTURE

If your profile looks like then then your posture is fundamentally correct, with all four key sockets lined up [*dashed yellow squares*]. A functional posture allows you to make a fundamentally solid swing, integrating proper weight transfer and body rotation. However, you must possess a balance of strength and flexibility in the various muscle groups in order to make a smooth motion as the muscles work together during your swing. Assuming that you possess ample strength and flexibility in this posture, you'll only need a maintenance program that will allow you to retain your current level of posture and function.

FORWARD POSTURE

This posture type—which is probably the most common—features hips, shoulders, and head leaning forward. A forward posture like this results when you're too tight in the front side of your body. What this means is that your anterior ("front-side") muscles have shortened and become too tight, pulling your body forward. Almost invariably, your muscles get this way from leading a sedentary lifestyle. A forward posture also can result from repeating certain sport motions (golf included) that require you to bend over to execute properly.

If this is your posture then it's highly likely that your abs and glutes are weak, which is unfortunate since these are the key muscles for stability and posture.

Unfortunately, most of us suffer changes in posture over time, due to a variety of factors including lifestyle, age, the type of sports we like to play and chosen vocation. These changes have a significant effect on what your body can and cannot do when you swing, mandating the need to make compensations in your setup and motion in order to execute a solid motion. On the following pages I'll describe the most common posture changes, and provide drills and setup adjustments you can make to improve your swing and the quality of your drives. First step: Identify your posture from the group below.

You'll learn a lot about your posture and how it affects your swing on the following pages, but this information covers only the tip of the iceberg. For everything you wanted to know about correct posture and flexibility in your swing, check out *Secrets of Golf Instruction and Flexibility* (Mountain Lion, $24.95), available at your favorite bookstore and amazon.com.

UNDER POSTURE

This posture type is defined simply as being weak and unstable. As you can see, the hips are tilted upward, indicating that there's not enough strength and support from the legs and hips. You'll tend to develop under posture when the powerful hip flexor muscles you rely on so heavily to support your upper torso simply become too weak to do their job. As a result, you must lean your head and shoulders forward to counterbalance the fact that your center of gravity has moved backward.

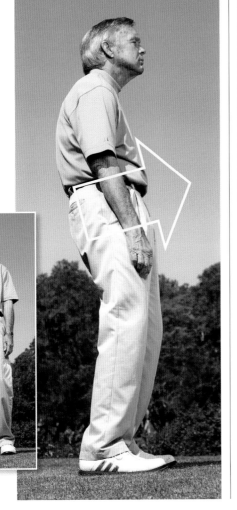

ROTATED POSTURE

This posture results from one side of your body getting too tight and out of balance with the other, causing your torso to rotate to one side. Very seldom do I see a person who doesn't have some degree of rotation like this in their posture, with an overwhelmingly number of golfers rotated to the left (i.e., the direction of their swing). As strange as this may seem, rotated posture usually results from hips that are tight and imbalanced. If you have a tight right hip, for example, it will almost invariably pull your right shoulder forward.

THE TUG OF WAR WITHIN YOUR SWING

I like to think of the swing as basically a tug of war between the 600-plus muscles in your body. Here's what I mean. As you shift your weight to your right side during your backswing, the muscles in the front of your right leg and hip contract (or load up). Meanwhile, the

muscles in the back of your right leg and hip simultaneously expand. The tug of war is on. The reverse happens in your torso: your upper-back muscles contract while the ones in front expand; and the muscles on the right side of your torso contract as the muscles on your left side expand.

And this is just in your backswing (everything switches roles as you come back down). You make your best swings when the tug of war ends in a tie—when your muscles do their jobs in balanced, equal amounts. Problem is, this never happens with anything but a functional posture.

The battle is on between contracting and expanding muscles (those in the front and right vs. those in the back and left) as you swing to the top and then back down.

If your posture is unable to compete in the tug of war then you'll make compensations that—unless perfectly timed—lead to errant drives that lack distance.

THE PROBLEM WITH FORWARD POSTURE

Common problems caused by a forward posture include difficulty "staying down" through the ball, a restricted shoulder turn and lack of power. This posture often forces you to raise up (causing a steep, over-the-top swing) and/or straighten your legs on the backswing and downswing.

The golfer with forward posture typically has difficulty staying down through the shot.

EFFECT 1:
Restricted Turn
Unlike a functional-posture golfer who's able to turn freely during the backswing and get the club parallel to the ground at the top, the player with forward posture is inhibited during his turn and, therefore, must stop the club at a spot just past vertical. This creates a lack of power and a steep downswing that often produces slices and fat shots.

EFFECT 2:
Over-the-Top Downswing
The functional-posture golfer is able to get the club on plane and attack the ball from the inside on the downswing. The player with forward posture is forced to come over the top, creating a lot of slices and pulls.

EFFECT 3:
Standing Up Through impact
The functional-posture golfer is able to stay in his posture through impact, allowing the club to attack on the desired, shallow angle. On the other hand, a golfer with forward posture is forced to stand up through impact, bringing his hips closer to the ball and sapping a ton of power from his swing.

HOW TO LIVE WITH YOUR FORWARD POSTURE

Address Position Adjustments

You can offset many of the ill effects of forward posture by simply altering your address position. Copy the setup here.

STRONGER GRIP
Strengthen your left hand grip to assist squaring and releasing the club through impact. Get the "V" formed by your left thumb and forefinger to point to your right shoulder.

DROP BACK
Since you have a difficult time rotating and allowing your muscles to move in sequence, drop your right foot back to create more shoulder turn. This will allow the club to swing deeper and attack the ball on a shallower angle.

FLARE OUT
Flare out both of your feet. This further increases your ability to rotate.

PLAY IT BACK
Moving the ball back in your stance will make it easier for you to hit down and through the shot with irons and assist in attacking the ball from the inside with the driver.

Try these practice drills to get the most out of your swing with a forward posture:

1. PULL BACK DRILL

What it does: Stops your tendency to stand up.

Step 1: Tee the ball up slightly with an 8-iron. Take your setup and pretend that you're standing in dried concrete and that your legs are completely frozen.

Step 2: Swing your arms and club into your finish position without moving your legs.

Step 3: From here, swing the club past the ball and up to the top of your backswing while keeping your lower body as braced as possible.

Step 4: From the top of your restricted backswing, swing your arms down through the ball. Make sure that you keep your right foot flat as you swing through.

The secret of this drill is to keep your right foot flat on the ground throughout your motion.

2. RIGHT-ARM ONLY DRILL

What it does: Teaches you to better square the face.

Step 1: Take out a mid-iron, and with your right arm only, try hitting a teed ball using your normal swing motion.

Step 2: Notice as you perform this drill how it's easier to square the clubface and release through impact (because you make a freer swing with only one hand on the handle). Replicate this feeling when you swing with both hands on the grip.

3. STEP ON THE GAS DRILL

What it does: Gives you power that a forward posture normally restricts.

Step 1: Pretend that there's a gas pedal under your left foot at address. For an enhanced effect, place a towel or other flat object where the gas pedal would be.

Step 2: As you start your downswing, step on the pedal (or towel) by getting at least 90 percent of your weight on your left foot before the club gets to the ball. To do this properly, shift your weight target-ward without allowing your upper body to move out in front of you.

THE PROBLEM WITH UNDER POSTURE

Because of the overall weakness in your lower body that comes with under posture, you're very likely an arms-and-hands swinger. As a result, you tend to lift the club during your backswing and then flail at the ball with your hands and arms coming down. This is a bad thing because power comes from coiling your upper body against your lower body, and you can't coil if you lift. Your bad shots include skulls, scuffs, shanks and very weak hits.

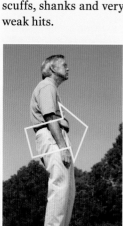

The weak lower body of a person with under posture makes generating power very difficult.

EFFECT 1: Lifting Instead of Turning

While a functional-posture golfer is able to rotate fully and get the club parallel to the ground at the top of the swing, the player with under posture can't and compensates by picking the club straight up in the air. The results are weak, slicing shots and an overall lack of power.

FUNCTIONAL

UNDER

EFFECT 2: A Need to Shift Laterally

Because of the lower body's inability to stabilize and support, an under-posture golfer should adopt a 2-plane swing, applying a lateral hip slide in the downswing to offset the lifting of the arms on the backswing.

UNDER

Z-PLANE

Address Position Adjustments

Imagine a quarterback in the grasp of a tackler who has him tight around his legs—this is you at the top of your backswing if you have under posture. You need to build power back into your motion, which you can do by copying the address positions below.

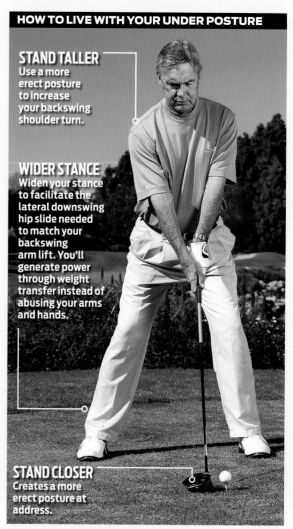

HOW TO LIVE WITH YOUR UNDER POSTURE

STAND TALLER
Use a more erect posture to increase your backswing shoulder turn.

WIDER STANCE
Widen your stance to facilitate the lateral downswing hip slide needed to match your backswing arm lift. You'll generate power through weight transfer instead of abusing your arms and hands.

STAND CLOSER
Creates a more erect posture at address.

Try these practice drills to get the most out of your swing with an under posture:

1. POWER FAN DRILL

What it does: Builds some power and strength back into your swing.

Step 1: Get into your setup with a power fan (available at most pro shops), then cock your wrists to set the fan just outside your right thigh with the fan parallel to the ground and to your target line.

Step 2: Pump the fan up to the top of your backswing and then swing it through to your finish, making it "whoosh" as it passes the left side of your body. The wings of the fan create resistance, so you're going to have to use some effort to really make it whoosh.

Practicing with a swing fan is one of the best ways to build strength and speed that's missing from your motion.

2. SET-TURN-PLACE DRILL

What it does: Teaches you to set the club without lifting it.

Step 1: Stand in a balanced address. While maintaining your posture, fold your arms and set the shaft of any club on your right shoulder.

Step 2: Keeping the shaft on your shoulder and staying in your spine angle, make a relaxed shoulder turn.

Step 3: Extend your arms away from your torso. This is where you should be at the top of your backswing.

3. BAG DRILL

What it does: How to use your legs instead of your arms.

Step 1: Take a normal address opposite an impact bag (a duffel stuffed with towels also does the trick).

Step 2: Swing into the bag, making sure to shift your weight forward. Really go after it! You'll know if you're incorrectly using your arms and hands or correctly driving with your hips and legs by the sound of your impact.

Hit the bag with leg power.

In addition to these three drills, also practice using the Pull Back drill from page 155.

THE PROBLEM WITH ROTATED POSTURE

If you have a rotated posture you tend to aim too far to the right in order to feel like you're squared up to the target line at setup. Also, because your right hip and shoulder are naturally set closer to the ball at address (most golfers with rotated posture are rotated to the left), you'll have a harder time turning away from the ball smoothly. The typical compensation in this scenario is to over-rotate your hips to assist your turning motion. When you do this you yank the club too far to the inside, setting up an over-the-top move coming down to the ball.

In the event you don't compensate by over-turning, you'll make the mistake of lifting the club, and you've seen the damage this move can do with the other two dysfunctional posture types.

Rotated posture is very common, and best fixed by executing the right kind of stretches to get you back to square.

EFFECT 1:
Poor Aim

Your right hip and shoulder are set closer to the ball than your left shoulder and hip in a rotated posture, making you feel like you're aiming to the left of the target even though you're square. You'll compensate (erroneously) by turning your stance to the right. When you do this, you're actually lining up right of the target, which in many instances automatically forces you to swing over the top. The fact that your right shoulder and hip are closer to the ball also makes approaching the ball from the inside difficult since this type of setup restricts a proper backswing turn.

EFFECT 2:
Spinning Out

A functional swinger is able to shift weight to the front side through impact. A player with rotated posture tends to strand weight on his right foot, causing the hips to spin out. Glancing blows and weak shots are the result.

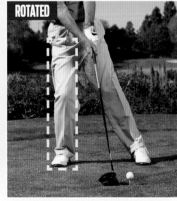

Address Position Adjustments

Although the ultimate goal is to restore the body back to balance and get the rotation out of your posture, a good way to compensate is to alter your setup. Copy the positions below.

STRONGER GRIP
Strengthen your left-hand grip and move the ball back in your stance.

CLOSE IT UP
Draw your right foot back in a closed position. Doing this will help you square your hips at address and allow you to turn your shoulders more during your backswing.

MAX ROTATION
To get the maximum amount of rotation from your lower body, flare out both feet at least 30 degrees to further enhance your hip turn in both directions.

HOW TO LESSEN ITS EFFECTS

Try these practice drills to get the most out of your swing with a rotated posture:

1. CLOSED STANCE DRILL

What it does: Helps you turn despite the natural blocking action of your right shoulder and hip. Good for power, too.

Step 1: Take your driver and assume a comfortable stance.

Step 2: Pull your right foot back and raise your heel so only the balls of your foot touch the ground.

Step 3: Take the club to the top and then swing down so you feel yourself attacking the ball from the inside.

2. LEFT-HANDED POWER FAN DRILL

What it does: Restores symmetry. Perform the same steps as on page 157, but this time swing the fan left-handed to work out the imbalance in your body rotation.

3. LEFT LEG PIVOT DRILL

What it does: Stops your "hang-back" move

Step 1: Take your address with the ball teed forward of your left foot. As you swing back, lift your left heel off the ground, transferring all of your weight to your right leg.

Step 2: Swing down by planting your left foot on the ground while simultaneously lifting up on your right toe. You'll really have to shift and get back to your left side to reach the forward ball position—a great feeling for a rotated golfer.

In addition to these three drills, also practice using the Step On the Gas drill from page 155.

Next Steps

If you're serious about getting your posture back to a functional state, follow the exercise protocols for each posture type at **golf.com/ bestdrivingbook.** You should perform these before engaging in your normal exercises program. Getting your body back into perfect posture is the first step in regaining your maximum anatomical function, and performing "standard" exercises isn't likely to get you back into alignment (more likely it'll make it worse.

Also, keep in mind that failing to achieve perfect posture immediately doesn't mean you're not getting closer to it, and the closer you are to it the more function you attain. I recommend that you perform the exercises and the swing drills on these pages five or six days a week—they're not very strenuous, and the more you perform them the more your body will learn what it's like to be in perfect posture.

Identifying your posture type provides you with important insight into not only your swing, but also your body because, as I tell my students, "Your body *is* your swing." Here's to a healthy life and healthier drives. ●

As you stretch to improve posture you're always one step closer toward perfect functionality.

Follow Roger's posture-improvement program at **golf.com/bestdrivingbook.**

5 THINGS TO TAKE FROM THIS CHAPTER

1 Even active golfers have to deal with structural and postural limitations. The problem is worse for golfers that lead a sedentary lifestyle.

2 There are ways to test your range of motion and improve it in key areas of your anatomy for a more efficient and dynamic swing.

3 Adjustments at address and during your motion can help you play better with a dysfunctional posture and limited range of motion.

4 To ultimately fix structural- and postural-limitation problems, engage in a proper stretching and conditioning program.

5 Every moment you spend improving your body brings you a step closer to where you want to be.

HIGH-TRACK/SLOT DRIVER
ALVARO QUIROS

If you want to hit it like the longest
Tour player, copy these moves

At 6'3", hard-swinging Spaniard Alvaro Quiros has quickly become the longest Tour professional in the world. Tiger Woods jokingly called Quiros "stupid long" at the 2009 PGA Championship. He continues to post a near 315-yard average.

One of the reasons Quiros is able to generate such eye-popping distance is, ironically, his setup, which features zero moving parts. His address position and posture are impeccable. With everything set so correctly at the start, Quiros can store up tremendous power and energy without worrying about his club and shaft falling off plane, which due to his height is the high-track shoulder plane [*Frame 4*].

Quiros makes a beautiful transition—he starts to unwind his hips without turning his shoulders, a move that drops his hands straight down [*Frame 7*]. More importantly, he performs these moves without losing his original setup tilt. The dropping action slots the club down to his right-arm plane and in perfect position to deliver the clubhead [*Frame 9*].

Three things that make Quiros's impact position so powerful: 1) His left leg has begun to straighten, 2) His hips are open to the target line but his shoulders are square, and 3) His right forearm and shaft are in line [*Frame 11*]. These are solid positions for any golfer. It doesn't get more powerful than this.

1

2

6

7

Sets the correct
kinetic sequence
in motion by
turning his hips
without spinning
his shoulders.

11

Straightens his
left leg right at
impact, causing
the club to smash
through with
whip-like speed.

12

KEY MOVE
Tracks to his natural plane (shoulder).

KEY MOVE
A perfect slot all the way down to the right-arm plane.

CHAPTER

9

The amount you can improve your driver swing is determined by the amount of time you dedicate to practicing it.

HOW TO *PRACTICE* YOUR DRIVER SWING

Once you discover how you should swing your driver it's time to put in the hours on the practice range to groove it for good

By **MIKE BENDER, PGA**
*Mike Bender Academy
Timacuan G.C., Lake
Mary, Fla.*
2009 Teacher
of the Year

ESTABLISHING YOUR DRIVING AS A strong part of your overall game relies on a combination of several factors, the most important of which is technique. If you've followed the previous chapters in this book closely, then you have a pretty good idea of how you should set up to the ball and which swing best matches your build, innate talents and physical limitations. Armed with this knowledge you can now begin implementing it on the practice tee and, eventually, on the course.

Because your driver is the longest club in your bag as well as the one with the least amount of loft and fastest speed, it gives you the smallest margin for error. This small margin demands that you swing your driver with a particular set of fundamentals or your consistency will suffer, and the only way to groove these fundamentals is to practice them.

Everyone who reads this book will dedicate different amounts of time toward applying the principles they've learned. The amount of time—in addition to the type of goals you set—goes a long way toward determining how much you'll improve. Some golfers don't have any time to practice except on the days that they play, while others have flexible enough schedules to practice on a regular basis. In order to avoid frustration, simply keep your expectations in line with the amount of time you plan to put into your improvement program (lower expectations for less practice and vice-versa).

The goal of anyone serious about improving should be to simplify his or her swing, and making it more efficient by eliminating excess movement. You do this with practice, but it has to be the right kind. Knowing *how* to practice and the keys that allow you to transfer your swing from the range to the course is crucial. It's important that you build feedback into every rehearsal session. In the best-case scenario this feedback takes the shape of an instructor. As it relates to this book, feedback comes in the form of the drills, training aids and practice stations outlined on the following pages, each of which are designed to let you know when you do something incorrectly as well as to create feels that will prove extremely beneficial to your swing.

There are six basic areas to consider when practicing your driver swing in order to maximize consistency and distance. They are as follows:

1. **Setup** (inclusive of aim, alignment, stance, posture, ball position and grip)
2. **Takeaway** (specifically, keeping the club on plane)
3. **Pivot** (the quality of your backswing turn)
4. **Delivery** (grooving the right path into the ball)
5. **Solid Contact** (nailing the sweet spot)
6. **Release** (guaranteeing that the clubface is square at the point of impact)

Grab your range tokens—it's time to improve your driving like never before.

WELCOME TO YOUR NEW PRACTICE STATION

In order to maximize your allotted practice time, I highly suggest that you construct and work from a practice station. A practice station will guide you through the correct motions in your swing and provide feedback if and when you stray from your fundamentals. You'll hit most of your practice shots with the drills in this chapter from your station. The question begs, "how many?" Before I lobby an answer, consider that it takes you about 1.5 seconds to complete each practice swing and that each time you visit the range you hit a large bucket, say 100 balls. That means you only practiced your swing for 150 seconds (1.5 x 100)—a whopping two and a half minutes! I'm not presenting this math to frustrate you, but to make sure you're aware that if you're serious about improving and playing better, you must get serious about practicing.

Here's how to build your station [*see graphic, opposite page*]:

1. Tee up a ball and mark this spot with a second tee set just six inches outside the first. You'll hit shots off the first tee and use the second to know exactly where to tee the next practice ball.

2. Place an alignment stick on the ground inside the second tee and point it at a target.

3. Construct a T-square. Visit your local D.I.Y shop and purchase three 1/2-inch PVC pipes, each 20" in length, and a PVC T-connector. Insert each of the three pieces of PVC pipe into the connector so that they form a larger "T." (The beauty of this tool is that you can easily break it down and stuff it in your bag.) Place the top of the T-square parallel to the alignment stick and the target line so that the stem runs between your feet when you take your stance.

4. Walk 10 yards out on your target line and set an aiming rod (with swim noodle affixed) in the ground in an upright position, directly in line with the target and the second tee.

Practicing Your Setup

The initial goal of the practice station is to help you build your address—you need to set up in the same way every time to create consistency in your swing. Each time you set up to hit shots in your practice station, look at the target and aiming rod (the upright shaft that you placed in the ground). Although the target will appear left of the aiming rod, in reality they're in perfect alignment. Always swing the club to the aiming rod, not the target.

Take your stance with both feet placed equidistant from the stem on the T, and use the top of the T and the alignments sticks on the ground to set your feet, knees, hips and shoulders parallel to your target line. A good idea is to place different-colored tape at different stance widths on the top of the T (widest for your driver) and distances from the ball on the stem of the T (furthest for your driver). This practice procedure will allow you to repeat your set up every time, paving the way to building a repeatable swing.

Testing Your Aim

Once you feel like you're properly set up in your station, bend down and lay the shaft of your club against your heels. Step away and lay a second shaft on the ground parallel to the heel line shaft and directly behind the ball. Where does this second shaft point? If it isn't at your intended target, your aim is off. Repeat this procedure until you can consistently dial in the correct aim. Your setup writes the script of how you're going to swing the club.

This bucket of 100 balls represents only 2.5 minutes of actual in-swing practice time.

REQUIRED ITEMS FOR PRACTICING YOUR DRIVER SWING

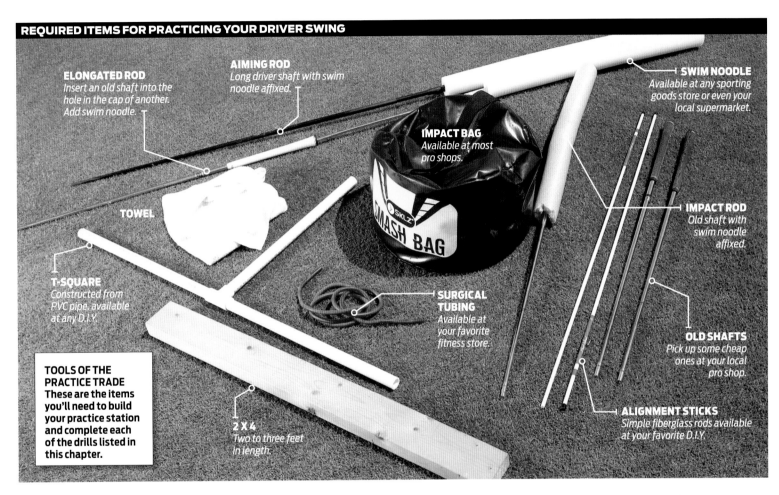

ELONGATED ROD
Insert an old shaft into the hole in the cap of another. Add swim noodle.

AIMING ROD
Long driver shaft with swim noodle affixed.

SWIM NOODLE
Available at any sporting goods store or even your local supermarket.

IMPACT BAG
Available at most pro shops.

TOWEL

IMPACT ROD
Old shaft with swim noodle affixed.

T-SQUARE
Constructed from PVC pipe, available at any D.I.Y.

SURGICAL TUBING
Available at your favorite fitness store.

OLD SHAFTS
Pick up some cheap ones at your local pro shop.

TOOLS OF THE PRACTICE TRADE
These are the items you'll need to build your practice station and complete each of the drills listed in this chapter.

2 X 4
Two to three feet in length.

ALIGNMENT STICKS
Simple fiberglass rods available at your favorite D.I.Y.

Now that your lower body is on line, check your upper body alignment. Set up in your station then place the shaft across your chest along your shoulder line. Without getting our of your address posture, use your eyes to verify that the shaft across your chest is parallel to the top of the T on the ground. This is critical to get right. Because you play the ball so far forward in your stance with a driver, it's easy for your shoulders to open up to the target line (point left of where you're aiming). Open shoulders will cause you to swing the club back to the outside, setting an over-the-top swing in motion. The opposite is true if your shoulders are closed.

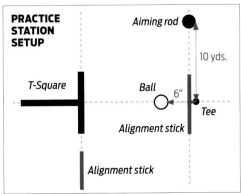

PRACTICE STATION SETUP

Aiming rod

10 yds.

T-Square

Ball

6"

Tee

Alignment stick

Alignment stick

Swing to the aiming rod despite the fact that it looks right of target when you take your stance.

"You need to set up in the same way every time to create consistency in your swing."

NOTE: If you make an error in alignment, it's better to do it with your feet aimed too far to the left and your shoulders aimed too far to the right. This alignment makes the target look like it's more to the right than it really is, influencing you to swing more to the right and creating the inside-out, ascending path necessary for maximum distance and accuracy.

HOW TO PRACTICE YOUR BACKSWING

Once you've learned to set up properly, taking the club back correctly and making a solid backswing will seem much easier. Don't confuse this, however, for automatic—you need to spend as much effort trying to groove this segment of your swing as you do on the others.

Tracking Drill

Location: Practice Station
Additional tools: Alignment stick (x2) and an old shaft
Grooves: A perfectly on-plane start to your swing

Set an alignment stick in line with the top of your T-square (you'll align your stance to this stick). Push another alignment stick through the hole in the cap of the grip on an old shaft, and then set the shaft at a 45-degree angle into the ground on your target line. Place the heel of your driver against the shaft and swing the club back at half speed, allowing the shaft of your driver to track up the shaft and then the stick. This is what an on-plane takeaway looks and feels like. Do this for ten swings, then step into your practice station and try to reproduce the same sensations.

Track your driver up a shaft set at a 45-degree angle to get a feeling for swinging back on plane.

Check your position at the halfway point of your backswing. If you're solid here than getting to the top should be easy.

Tracking Drill with Resistance

Location: Practice Station
Additional tools: Alignment stick and old shaft; Surgical tubing
Grooves: A perfectly on-plane start to your swing

To accelerate your learning with the Tracking Drill, add a 3-foot piece of surgical tubing to the process. Step on one end of the tubing with your left foot and secure the other end between your left hand and the grip of your club. The tubing should be fairly taut. Begin swinging the club back along the pole until you reach the top of your backswing. As you do this you'll notice that the resistance from the tubing increases the closer you get to the top of your swing. Do this for ten swings, then step into your practice station and try to reproduce the same sensations. The resistance enhances the learning process, making the experience more dramatic and permanent.

"Once you've learned to set up properly, taking the club back correctly and making a solid backswing will seem much easier. "

Repeat the Tracking Drill with a piece of surgical tubing that runs from your grip to under your left foot.

The resistance provided by the tubing doubles the effectiveness of the Tracking Drill.

HOW TO PRACTICE YOUR PIVOT

Taking the club back on plane is only part of the story. Making the biggest and most fundamentally sound turn away from the ball you can will give your swing the potential energy it needs for an explosive impact.

Turning and getting your hands to the wall at the top of your swing without disturbing your forward tilt puts you in a solid position to swing back down to the ball.

Start.

Posture Maintenance Drill

Location: Interior or exterior wall
Additional tools: None
Grooves: Proper backswing turn

Once the proper forward and secondary tilts are in place at address [*see Spine Tilt Check, below*], your goal is to turn around your spine without disturbing them as you bring the club to the top. Take your setup without a club and with your rear end just touching a wall and your eyes fixated on the spot on the ground where the ball would be. Turn your hips and shoulders using your normal motion and swing your hands up to the top, making sure they contact the wall at the end of your backswing. If you're able to reach this position without moving out of your address posture (altering your forward or secondary tilt), then you've achieved several prerequisites of an effective swing. From here you're in perfect position to accelerate the clubhead toward the ball with your arms on the proper angle.

Spine Tilt Check

Location: Anywhere
Additional tools: None
Grooves: The correct spine tilts at address

Because the ball is on the ground it's necessary to tilt your upper body forward from your hip joints to reach it. Also, because your right hand sits lower on the handle than your left, you have to tilt your upper body away from the target. To encourage the proper tilts, hold the grip end of your driver against your sternum and bend forward from your hips like you're addressing a ball. Next, angle your upper body to the right until the shaft touches your left leg. This is how much tilt you should feel in your setup position.

Start.

Tilt right.

Perfect.

Base Rotation Drill

Location: Interior or exterior wall
Additional tools: None
Grooves: The correct feeling of turning around your spine

Stand 12 inches from a wall (eyes toward it), cross both arms across your chest, and bend forward from your hips until your forehead contacts the wall (wearing a hat helps). Now turn your shoulders in both directions continuously while trying to maintain contact with the wall with your forehead.

This seemingly simple drill is important because the better your body can turn around its axis (your spine), the more efficient and consistent your swing will be. Physics states that objects move fastest at right angles to their axis (remember how much faster the tether ball traveled around the pole when it was high in the air versus when it was low?). Therefore, it's essential that your axis is positioned correctly at the start and that you can maintain it during your turn back and through.

NO!

If your forehead moves off the wall then you destroyed any chance of maximizing speed.

Start here.

YES!

End here.

Turn your shoulders and hips back and through while keeping your forehead in constant contact with the wall to practice maintaining your forward tilt.

Posture & Plane Maintenance Drill

Location: Exterior wall
Additional tools: Towel
Grooves: Proper backswing body motion and an on-plane backswing

Perform the Posture Maintenance Drill at left, but this time using a club and with a towel tucked between your upper arms and your chest. If the club makes contact with the wall when you go to swing, then your backswing is off plane. Practice this drill until you can swing to the top without hitting the wall. The towel is under your arms to stop you from lifting your arms or the club. If it drops, you cheated.

Start here.

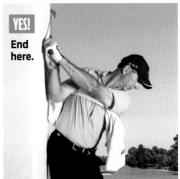

YES!

End here.

Swing back without colliding with the wall.

NO!

The towel knows if you've cheated by lifting your arms to avoid contacting the wall.

Start here.

Maintain both points of contact (right ear and left hip) as you take the club back...

...and also as you bring it back down. Doing so encourages proper body action.

Secondary Spine Tilt Maintenance Drill

Location: Practice Station
Additional tools: Elongated rod and impact rod
Grooves: Proper backswing and downswing body positions

Stick the elongated rod with swim noodle into the ground opposite your right hip and just beyond your target line as shown, and your impact rod straight into the ground against the outside your left instep. Make sure that the swim noodle on the elongated rod rests against your right ear as you settle into your address position with your upper body correctly leaning away from the target. Hit some shots (start with teed 7-iron, progressing all the way up to your driver) with the primary goal of keeping your right ear in contact with the noodle throughout your swing and well past impact. Maintaining this contact guarantees that the spine angles you establish at address aren't lost during your swing.

Simultaneously, keep your left hip in contact with the impact rod placed next to your left hip. These two points of contact (right ear and left hip) enhance your ability to swing your arms and club into the ball from the right direction without having to make compensations.

If your right ear comes off the noodle on your right during your backswing you're guilty of reverse pivoting with a slice being the likely result.

If your left hip comes off the noodle to your left during your downswing you're in a very poor position to deliver the club on plane and with sufficient force.

BONUS DRILL

Connect Your Pivot

To really sharpen up your pivot action, hit shots with a towel under both arms. Set the towel between your upper arms and chest [*photo, below*], and simply swing back and through, trying to make as solid contact as you can without the towel falling to the ground. You'll instantly feel how you must pivot your body more than swing your arms to keep the towel in place. Use only a three-quarter swing. Start with a teed 7-iron and progress all the way up to your driver.

HOW TO PRACTICE YOUR DELIVERY

ecause you stand farthest from the ball when you're swinging your driver, your delivery must be much shallower than with your other clubs. If you can get your arms to travel more around your body, then making a shallower downswing is actually a lot easier than you might think.

The following drills are designed to alleviate two of the most common downswing errors: swinging over-the-top and swinging over-the-bottom. To understand these mistakes, split your downswing into two equal parts. If your hands shift out toward the target and the shaft doesn't drop down behind you to compensate, your approach will be too steep and over the top. Similarly, if all is well until the bottom half of the downswing and the shaft tips out toward the ball improperly ("over the bottom"), your results also will be undesirable. If you are "over the top" and "over the bottom" in an exaggerated manner, use one of your mid-irons off the tee because hitting your driver will be nearly impossible.

Adjusting your Practice Station to give you the best possible feedback on the quality of your delivery isn't difficult and will immediately make your practice time ultra-effective. First, reset the Tracking Drill setup [page 168], track up the shaft and re create your best top-of-the-backswing position. Make sure your left arm is positioned at a right angle to your spine—you must be fundamentally solid here before attempting any of the delivery drills on this and the opposite page. Use a mid-iron and periodically pick up your driver, swinging it in a similar manner, until you can mimic the position in the photo at right every time.

Practice getting your left arm at a right angle to your spine at the top before attempting the delivery drills.

The Practice Station setup to fix an over-the-top swing.

Over-The-Top Drill

Location: Practice Station
Additional tools: Elongated rod; old shaft; impact rod
Grooves: Proper delivery without coming over the top

Push the elongated rod into the hole in the cap of an old shaft, then set the shaft in the ground at a 45-degree angle as shown. Take your address position so that the noodle barely rests on your right shoulder, then step slightly away from the target, creating a gap of approximately one inch between the noodle and your shoulder. Have a friend tee a ball in front of your driver and mark the spot with a second tee for reference.

Make slow practice backswings while tying to get your left arm in the correct position at the top of your backswing. If you bump the shaft then your left arm is too high. Add the impact rod to the drill, setting it at the same 45-degree angle as the elongated rod as shown. Repeat your backswing as above, but this time add your downswing. If you can swing to the top without hitting the elongated rod and come back to the ball without hitting the impact rod, then it's impossible for you to come over the top.

Over-The-Bottom Drill

Location: Practice Station
Additional tools: Impact rod
Grooves: Proper deliver without swinging too far under plane

Set the impact rod into the ground at the angle shown below. The swim noodle should only be a foot off the ground. Get into your address position opposite the foam end of the rod, touch the noodle with the top of your shaft and then shuffle backward to create approximately three inches of clearance between the foam and your club. Take one step toward the target and put the tee in the ground at the driver head's position. Mark this spot with a tee and set your T-square in the middle of your stance.

Begin swinging back and through making sure your driver travels under the foam during your backswing and, more importantly, on the downswing. If the shaft gets too steep coming into the impact area you'll make contact with the noodle—immediate (and harmless) feedback that you tipped the clubhead out. Continue without a ball until successful and then proceed to hit actual shots at slow speed with the goal of hitting the ball roughly half of your normal distance. Gradually ramp up your speed as your success dictates.

As you progress with this drill you'll notice that as you swing into the ball on the proper path your hands will need to release to achieve any sort of consistency. Every golfer develops release habits based on the path that they use to deliver the club to the ball. Since most golfers swing into the ball too steeply they use their hands to deliver the clubface in an open position to compensate. For this reason it is necessary to fix the path first and then adjust or develop the correct release to produce a consistent ball flight.

Delivery Check Drill

Location: Practice Station
Additional tools: Impact rod
Grooves: Proper downswing body positions and an on-plane delivery

Set the impact rod at the same angle as the lie angle of the club you're swinging (begin this drill with a teed 7-iron then progress all the way up to your driver). Set the rod about a foot outside the target line and two feet to the right of the ball. Make waist-high to waist-high swings (eventually progressing to full swings). Your goal is to swing under the shaft from start to finish. If you come over the top or swing too far from over the bottom your driver shaft will crash into the noodle. Remember to change the impact rod angle whenever you switch to a different club.

HOW TO PRACTICE MAKING SOLID CONTACT

With your backswing and downswing in decent shape, it's time to build some good habits as they relate to making consistent contact in the center of your driver's sweet spot. The following two drills do a great job of blending what you've practiced in your backswing and downswing with some weight shift and face-squaring needs, giving you the extra "pop" you require to reach new parts of the fairway.

Square Face Drill
Location: Practice tee
Additional tools: None
Grooves: A square face at the point of contact

Address a teed ball with your driver and swing the club back by moving your left arm across your chest without turning your hips. Hinge the club with your wrists so that the grip points at the target line when your left arm is parallel to the ground. From this position, simply rotate your hips and deliver the clubhead into the back of the ball. Perform this drill in slow motion at first. As you get better at squaring the clubhead at impact (i.e., hitting the ball straight) and making solid contact, increase your tempo (but not the length of your swing).

You can't make solid impact—or the right kind of divot—with your weight on your right foot. Get it left and watch the ball explode.

Target Side Drill
Location: Practice tee
Additional tools: Towel
Grooves: A proper strike with your weight on your front leg while rotating through the shot

Place a towel on the ground perpendicular to your target line as shown. Arrange a row of balls an inch or two in front of the towel (on the target side) and start blasting away with any of your mid-irons—your goal is to strike each ball without snagging the towel, making a divot right in front of it. This drill trains you to get your weight on your left foot at impact (if you're snagging the towel then your weight isn't as far forward as it needs to be). If you have difficulty with this drill, use half-swings and increase them in size and speed only after you're able to make 10 correct divots in a row.

HOW TO PRACTICE YOUR RELEASE

Powering the club through the hitting area and into your release so that you catch the ball with a square clubface every time is all about rotating your fore-arms counter-clockwise and turning the knuckles of your left hand down as you come into impact. The amount of rotation needed depends on the type of grip you use. For example, past Masters champion Zach Johnson, who I teach, has a very strong grip. He needs much less forearm and wrist rotation to deliver the clubface properly than someone who uses a weaker grip, like another student of mine Jonathan Byrd. Obviously both release styles work, but the drills described here are meant to take advantage of a neutral grip since that's what most golfers use.

Bowed-to-Flat Drill

Location: Practice tee
Additional tools: None
Grooves: Solid wrist action through impact (no collapsing or flipping)

Take your regular grip and then slide your right hand up the handle until the all the fingers on your right hand overlap those on your left. Make your normal swing, but as you approach impact use your right hand to pull the knuckles of your left hand into a bowed position.

As you swing down through the impact area, turn the knuckles of your left hand towards the ground (down). This is the way good players release the club.

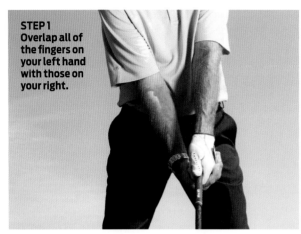

STEP 1
Overlap all of the fingers on your left hand with those on your right.

STEP 2
Make your regular swing.

STEP 3
Use your right-hand fingers to pull your left wrist into a bowed position as you swing into impact.

STEP 4
Continue through impact with a bowed left wrist.

STEP 5
Release by flattening your left wrist while turning your left-hand knuckles toward the ground.

Watch a video of this important drill with Top 100 Teacher Mike Bender at **golf.com/bestdriving book**

IF THE BAG SPINS TO THE LEFT... You've approached the ball from the outside using the over-the-top swing you can't afford to make.

IF THE BAG SPINS TO THE RIGHT... You've correctly approached the ball from the inside. This is the goal of the drill: get the bag to spin out to the right.

If continued attempts don't yield desired results, slow down and proceed with one arm at a time until the bag is moving in the correct direction with each arm. Then use both arms together again and the bag should move correctly.

Impact Bag Drill

Location:
Practice Station
Additional tools:
Impact bag
Grooves:
An inside-path with a closing clubface through impact

Place an impact bag (available at most pro shops) or a duffel bag full of old towels where the ball would be and set a shaft in the ground on the target side of the bag right up against it. Make sure the center of the bag, the shaft behind it and your aiming rod all line up. Take your regular address making sure you align your body parallel to your target line, then swing back and through, catching the bag at three-quarter speed. The shaft behind the bag will cause it to spin one way or the other depending on the quality of your path and release [*see captions, above*].

Replace the bag, but this time focus on contacting the bag with the toe of your club well before the heel section.

Imagine that the toe is a razor-sharp point. Your goal is to stab the bag while also getting it to rotate to the right of the shaft. This face rotation is necessary to spin the ball back to the target in a right-to-left movement. Once you have it, you've achieved perfection: an inside path and a squaring clubface. Although this may seem like an exaggeration of the desired clubface position, when speed is added it's likely that you'll need to exaggerate closing of the clubface, especially if you've suffered from swinging out-to-in and a slice ball flight. Alternate between hitting the bag and then a few practice balls. You'll quickly ingrain the feel that produces the best results.

Set up to slam the board.

Make a slow-motion impact while squaring the clubface to the board.

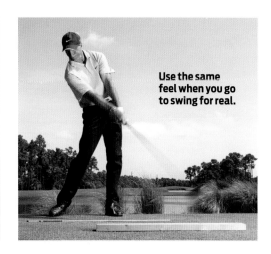

Use the same feel when you go to swing for real.

Impact Rehearsal Drill

Location: Practice Station
Additional tools: 2 x 4
Grooves: Pairing the correct delivery with the right amount of clubface rotation

Position the sawed end of a 2 x 4 where the ball would be and make slow-motion practice swings into the board with the clubface stopping flush to the edge. Just like the Impact Bag drill, this exercise gets you into the good habit of delivering the club on the correct inside path with the proper re-squaring of the clubface. Make five of these slow-motion practice swings to the 2 x 4, then move the board out of the way and hit two drives at half speed. Repeat this drill multiple times moving the board in and out of the hitting area until you're consistently hitting solid draws.

Message Drill

Location: Anywhere
Additional tools: None
Grooves: Awareness of the squaring action of your left hand

You won't need a club for this one. Get into your address position and make a mock swing with your left arm only. Stop when your arm reaches waist height in your follow-through and open your palm. You should be able to see the center of your palm, or better yet, read a message written on the underside of your glove. The checkpoint is that at this stage in your swing your palm should be facing up toward you, and you can only achieve this position if you bow your left wrist through impact. ●

5 THINGS TO TAKE FROM THIS CHAPTER

1 A proper setup allows you to make a proper turn.

2 A proper turn allows you to deliver the clubhead to the ball on a shallower angle.

3 Approaching the ball on a shallower path allows you to engage the proper release.

4 The sequence of these motions are what produce long and accurate drives.

5 Each step in the sequence can be practiced and grooved to build a swing you can trust and use to enjoy the game more.

TAKE YOUR PRACTICE TO A NEW LEVEL: ACTIVITY-SPECIFIC TRAINING

By **CHRIS WELCH**
ZenoLink
Endicott, N.Y.

Some teachers believe that the best way for their students to improve is to practice traditional drills with a ball, a club and some training aids. Others feel strongly that increasing strength and flexibility through a physical training regimen is the way to go. While both of those methods have their merits, I've found that the best way to improve performance is to combine the two philosophies by training the body in ways that duplicate golf-specific patterns and movements.

Improving your golf-specific coordination will teach your body to move in the patterns necessary for a sound motion (i.e., the proper sequence), thereby making your swing more efficient and effective. This can be done through a **Progressive Skills Training program**, the basics of which are:

1. Create a solid base with your lower body. To do this you have to learn to "grip" the ground firmly and rotate your body without letting go of this connection.

2. Learn how to engage your core muscles and stabilize your spine while firmly connecting to the ground and rotating your body.

3. Learn to swing your driver around a stable core and a connected lower body. Your arms must remain relaxed while your lower body and core remain stable. This allows the

club to be accelerated with great speed and relatively little effort.

Progressive Skills Training doesn't replace fitness training or swing instruction, but instead ties the two together. The most effective way to approach this aspect of training is in phases, completed over the course of 20 weeks.

Phase 1 focuses on skill development and re-training certain aspects of your swing-movement pattern based on your bio-

mechanical strengths and weaknesses [*see exercises, next page*]. This phase generally lasts 8 weeks.

Phase 2 focuses on speed development through movement pattern [*see exercises, page 181*]. This phase, again, lasts 8 weeks.

Phase 3 is geared more toward in-season training. Emphasis is placed on maintaining off-season gains while targeting areas for improvement utilizing a combination of exercises from the previous phases.

Blending classic practice regimens with fitness training is a new method for enhancing performance.

Core Separation with Swiss Ball

What it does: Teaches you to coil your upper body against a stable lower body.

How to do it: Place a Swiss ball between your legs and fold your arms across your chest, holding your driver along your shoulder line as shown. Rotate your torso back and forth while keeping your feet firmly connected to the ground. Make sure you maintain your balance.

Turn this.

Not this.

Towel Snap with Swiss Ball

What it does: Teaches you to brace your lower body before impact so you can deliver your club to the ball more efficiently and with more speed.

How to do it: Place a Swiss ball between your legs and swing back to the top with both hands on a towel. Swing down and try to snap the towel at the ball (or impact bag) as you reach impact.

Train pulling with your left hand while pushing with your right.

Lead Arm Swing/Trail Arm Push with Swiss Ball

What it does: Coordinates both the pushing and pulling components of your swing. By doing so it promotes greater acceleration of the clubhead through the ball.

How to do it: Place a Swiss ball between your legs and grip the club with your right hand open but pressed firmly against the grip. Swing back and then down into an impact bag, pushing the club with your right hand while simultaneously pulling it with your left. Deliver the club into the bag by straightening your right arm fully.

Swing from a dead stop to engage your core and speed.

Short-Response Plyometric Swings

What it does: Develops a faster swing by engaging the core with lower body acceleration.

How to do it: Take your driver and assume a backswing so your arms are horizontal to the ground. From a dead stop, swing aggressively through to the release. This can be done in the air or into an impact bag.

Long-Response Plyometric Swings

What it does: Promotes a faster swing by placing additional stress on your muscles during these training swings.

How to do it: Start with your driver pointed toward the target and swing back quickly into your regular top postion. As your arms become horizontal to the ground, begin swinging forward aggressively and into the finish. This can be done in the air or with an impact bag.

Elongated swings stress your muscles to increase their strength.

Swing an adjustable-weight club, alternating between light and heavy, or...

...swing with a towel tied around the hosel to build strength...

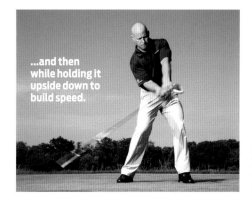

...and then while holding it upside down to build speed.

Under-Speed and Over-Speed Training

What it does: Builds strength and speed in equal amounts and at the same time

How to do it: You can do this with an adjustable-weight club or by applying and removing weights to your driver, but a towel also does the trick. The key is to alternate swinging a heavier club (for strength) and a lighter club (for speed). Wrap the towel around the hosel and make five swings, then remove it and swing the club five times held upside down. Alternate repeatedly.

For more information on these exercises and Phase 3, visit visit zenolink.com and **www.golf.com/bestdriving book.**

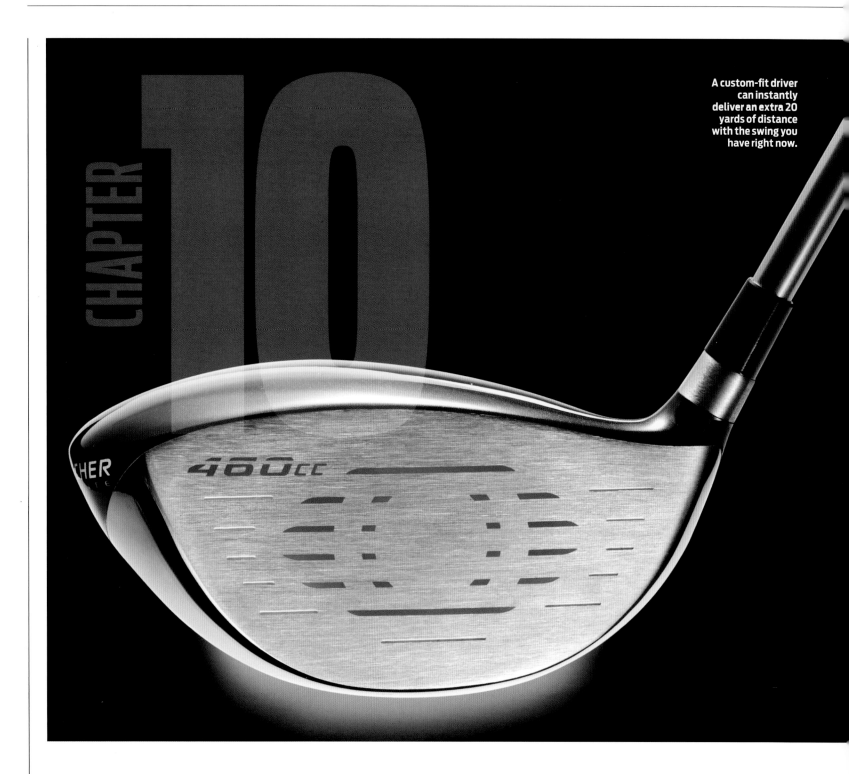

A custom-fit driver can instantly deliver an extra 20 yards of distance with the swing you have right now.

CHAPTER **10**

460cc

HOW TO FIND *YOUR* PERFECT DRIVER

Your body determines your swing. Your swing determines your gear. Here's all you need to know to match them perfectly by dialing in the correct set of specs.

By **CHRIS DEMPSEY** *&*
KEVIN WALKER, PGA
Fuzion Golf, Jupiter, Fla.

YOUR ABILITY TO MAXIMIZE YOUR LENGTH off the tee with a high percentage of accuracy comes down to perfecting the delivery of the club into to the back of the ball with a perfectly fit weapon. There's a chance that you can compensate for a driver that doesn't fit you; however, maximizing the frequency in which all the stars align using an off-the-rack club is a daunting task at best. A properly matched clubhead design and shaft—and correct assembly of these two items—provide you with a much better shot.

Most of the pages in this book have been dedicated to finding and owning your driver-swing fundamentals. Once you master these, you'll need a club that's a perfect match to you and your new motion. The key steps are thus: Match your swing to your body, then match your driver to your swing. Of course, you have to do your part—a repeating technique is key. A properly fit and built driver, however, makes repeatability easier to achieve. It can instantly dial in your optimal launch angle, spin rate, ball speed, efficiency and, therefore, distance and accuracy.

First Steps

If you're serious about improving your driving game and wish to take it as far as it can go with custom-fit gear, your first course of action is to determine your fitting preference and your goals. There are two different ways to get fit for a driver:

DEVELOPMENTAL FITTING
"Fit me to where I can truly maximize my potential"
A developmental fitting is for someone who's attempting to change something about his or her technique or ball flight through proper instruction and equipment testing. This person is taking lessons, quantifying their improvement and understands why they're making a change.

CORRECTIVE FITTING
"Maximize where I am right now"
A corrective fitting is for someone who wants to be fit to optimize his or her efficiency based on current swing characteristics. This person plays casually, never practices and—honestly—doesn't plan to.

In other words, you can be fit to push your current technique to where you ultimately want to go, or be fit to match the technique you have at present. Either of these fitting types works perfectly—it's up to you to figure out which one you prefer. As the saying goes, "the choice is yours." The important thing is that you make one. Through years of experience both teaching the game and fitting, testing and building equipment, we can honestly report that if you're playing with an off-the-rack driver then you're leaving at least an extra 20—and possibly dozens more—yards on the table.

CHOOSE YOUR FITTING STYLE

When finally deciding on the type of fitting that's right for you, keep in mind that a developmental fitting could require some "break-in time" with your new driver, and that you'll have to trust and understand that it will perform better as your technique improves. A correctional fitting provides much more instant gratification, but with the caveat that your driver will only be able to do so much since your mechanics don't produce the maximum efficiency.

Take this quick test to see which type of fitting you should opt for based on where you are right now with your driving game.

1. Timing
a. I want to drive the ball better right now!
b. I'm willing to wait if it pays off.

2. Commitment to Practice
a. I'm lucky to find enough time to watch golf on TV let alone practice or play.
b. I practice as much as I play.

3. Swing Knowledge
a. I don't want to think about my swing. Too many thoughts confuse me.
b. I want to know my swing inside and out, how it works, and its strengths and weaknesses.

4. Outlook
a. The handicap I have today is probably the one I'll have next year and 10 years down the road.
b. I'm playing below my potential. I feel like I can become a much better golfer.

5. Swing Style
a. Do I have one?
b. I have one, but it's time to try something else.

6. Reason for Playing
a. I enjoy the time with my friends, and would enjoy it more if I could hit a few more fairways.
b. I love the challenge and want to score lower every time I tee it up.

ADJUST
Moveable hosels allow fitters to dial in face angle for straighter hits with a faulty swing.

GO LIGHT
Don't balk if you're directed to a lighter-weight driver head—it might go longer.

SAVE FACE
A driver built with the maximum allowable C.O.R. in the face is key to max out your Smash Factor.

LAUNCHER ULTRALITE

If you answered A more than you did B to these questions then you're a likely candidate for a corrective fitting. Remember, neither option is better than the other. A corrective fitting actually is a very powerful tool. There are plenty of head and shaft combinations that can instantly improve your launch angle and spin rate to limit the amount of curvature, and increase your distance with the swing you own right now. The important thing is that you enter a fitting—whichever one it turns out to be—knowing what you're trying to get out of it and with a realistic idea of what you can achieve.

QUANTIFY YOUR DATA

Whether you're serious about a fitting or not, it's important to find out what you're getting out of your swing right now. At the very least you should discover the basic data behind your motion. Launch monitors like FlightScope® and TrackMan™ (two of the best) have become powerful tools for fitting and instruction. They not only provide important information about how your tee ball flies through the air, but also how you're delivering the club. Launch monitors allow clubfitters and instructors to quantify data so they can maximize efficiency.

Some monitors measure just a short distance of the overall ball flight and extrapolate the final data through very precise algorithms. Others apply a Doppler radar to measure the entire ball flight. Regardless, it's critical to have one present when being fit for your driver (or to just gain some inside knowledge on your swing), and to trust the person using the information to determine the best driver combination for you.

When you're on a launch monitor you should know exactly what's being measured. The following eight parameters are widely considered the most important to look out for:

1. LAUNCH ANGLE

The initial angle at which the ball leaves the face
Launch angle is affected by the loft of the club, clubface angle (open or closed) and your angle of attack. Typically, you want to achieve high launch and low spin for max distance.

Highest on PGA Tour: 14.25 degrees
Average on PGA Tour: 10.72 degrees

2. SPIN RATE

The number of revolutions per minute the ball makes as it spins backwards
Spin rate is affected by the loft of the club, the weight of the shaft (in grams), the flex of the shaft (measured in cycles per minute), your angle of attack (ascending, flat or descending), clubface angle (open or closed), shaft profile (tip-stiff, butt-stiff, tip-soft), shaft torque and the ball type. The longest drivers are typically those that produce the least amount of spin and the proper launch. If you're a slower swinger, however, you may need more spin to get the ball up.

Lowest on PGA Tour: 2,197.5 rpm
Average on PGA Tour: 2,655.4 rpm

3. SMASH FACTOR

An efficiency rating based on your ball speed versus your clubhead speed
Smash Factor determines how solidly you make contact with the ball. It's measured by dividing

"Enter a fitting knowing what you're trying to get out of it and with a realistic idea of what you can achieve."

FACE ANGLE
Many non-adjustable clubs have slightly closed clubfaces, providing more actual loft.

your ball speed by your clubhead speed (if your clubhead speed is 100 mph and your ball speed is 120 mph, then your Smash Factor is 1.2). A perfectly efficient Smash Factor is 1.5. If you begin to see Smash Factors of greater than 1.50 then it's likely that the head of your driver is above the maximum C.O.R. (Coefficient of Restitution) measurement allowed by the USGA.

The rub is that the slower you swing the more difficult it becomes to produce ball speeds fast enough to create an efficient Smash Factor. It's the same story if your clubhead speed is extremely high. Regardless, the key to getting as close as possible to Smash Factor efficiency is consistently catching the ball on the sweet spot of your driver.

Slow Swing Inefficiency
Clubhead speed: 75 mph
Ball speed needed for 1.5 Smash Factor: 112.5 mph
This is physically impossible.

Fast Swing Inefficiency
Clubhead speed: 135 mph
Ball speed needed for 1.5 Smash Factor: 202.5 mph
This requires an illegal clubhead

Highest on PGA Tour: *1.486*
Average on PGA Tour: *1.478*

4. CLUBFACE ANGLE
A measurement (in degrees) of how open or closed the clubface is to the target at impact
Clubface angle is affected by the timing of your swing, shaft flex relative to clubhead speed, hand speed, how you load the shaft and the shaft profile. There isn't a perfect measurement of clubface angle by itself, but there's one relative to your clubhead path. For years it was believed and taught that clubface angle determined curvature, while clubhead path determined starting direction. We now know that starting direction is mostly determined by clubface angle and curvature is determined by the clubface angle relative

to path. For example, if your clubhead travels through impact on a line that's 3 degrees from inside the target line and your clubface angle is 1.5 degrees open, the ball will start just right of the target and draw back. Yes, the face is open, but it's actually 1.5 degrees closed relative to the path, creating draw spin.

In a more typical example, if your clubhead travels through impact on a line that's 5 degrees from outside the target line (over-the-top swing) with your face angle 2.5 degrees closed, the ball will start just left of the target and then slice. The face is closed, but it's actually 2.5 degrees open relative to the path, creating slice spin. (For more on this consult the D-Plane models in Chapter 1.)

> **"Sticking with a driver based on its looks without knowing the numbers others could produce for you isn't very smart."**

LOOKS
You may want a club that looks good from this view at address, but go with the one that gives you the best numbers.

5. CLUBHEAD PATH
The path on which the club is swung on relative to the target
A positive path number means you swung the club in-to-out. A negative path number describes an out-to-in swing. Path is affected by club length, lie angle, your physical weaknesses and strengths, and shaft flex. If you want maximum distance, you need to deliver your driver into the ball from inside the target line.

6. CLUBHEAD SPEED
A measurement (in miles per hour) of how fast the club is moving at impact
Clubhead speed is affected by club length, shaft flex, hand speed, swing technique, overall club weight and your athleticism. Although clubhead speed is a critical component of distance, quality of contact is still more important.

Highest on PGA TOUR: *125.34 mph*
Average on PGA Tour: *112.68 mph*

7. BALL SPEED
The speed (in miles per hour) at which the ball initially leaves the clubface after impact
Ball speed is affected by solidity of contact, clubhead speed, shaft flex, C.O.R. of the driver and the type of ball you use. You need to get this combination right to max out ball speed.

Highest on PGA Tour: *185.80 mph*
Average on PGA Tour: *166.61 mph*

8. ANGLE OF ATTACK
The angle on which the clubhead approaches the ball relative to the ground at impact
Angle of attack is affected by the swing weight of the club, shaft flex, swing method and clubhead path. Generally, longer hitters have a positive angle of attack (0 to 7 degrees) and shorter, more controlled hitters are generally closer to 0 or even slightly negative (0 to -3 degrees). Basically, if you want to hit the ball long, hit it on the upswing.

HOW CLUBHEADS DIFFER AND HOW TO CHOOSE THE RIGHT ONE FOR YOU

If you're serious about getting the most out of your gear, it's important that you go into the fitting process with an open mind. We understand brand loyalty. However, the manufacturer you traditionally support might not always supply the most efficient combination of specs for you. Every manufacturer reports that their products produce the best launch, best spin, highest maximum C.O.R., best ball speed, etc. You need to test them all on a launch monitor to see for yourself. Again, it boils down to your numbers—maximizing these is the goal.

If you love the look of your driver, and that look gives you confidence, great. But sticking with it without knowing the numbers other drivers could potentially produce for you just isn't very smart. **We've found over the years that when a driver fitting is performed correctly, golfers always opt for the combination that gives them the best numbers regardless of brand.** That doesn't mean that one driver works for everybody. Every golfer has their own unique way of delivering the club, and what works for your buddy may not work for you. It's critical that you find a clubfitter who's brand-agnostic, totally performance based and quantifies your numbers using a launch monitor.

Once your fitter knows your swing and ball-flight tendencies, he or she should be able to narrow down your head choices based on your numbers, your fitting type and your goals. You won't be asked to test 30 different driver heads. Instead, you'll likely agree on a couple designs that perform the most efficiently and give you the best numbers, then begin tuning up the engine that actually runs them: the shaft

FINE TUNE
Some new drivers can be adjusted for lie angle, loft and face angle right on the spot.

SIZE
Bigger clubheads have made driving the ball easier in many respects, but require extra control from the right type of shaft.

SHAFTS & HOW THEY WORK

Once you narrowed down the best clubhead design for you it's time to really maximize it. Don't allow yourself to be satisfied using the stock shaft that comes with your driver. Proper club-fitters will have thousands of combinations of heads and shafts. And with the interchangeability that exists now, the options are endless.

1. Shaft Weight

Today's driver shafts range in weight from 30 to 125 grams. Some companies are using technology that make a 40-gram shaft play like an 80-gram shaft. The lighter the shaft the more the ball will spin (the opposite is true for heavier shafts).

2. Shaft Profile

The profile of the shaft allows your fitter to accomplish many things during a fitting. Tweaking this spec can help you more consistently square the clubface, launch the ball higher, spin the ball less and swing faster. It can also hinder from doing these things just as easily. Because a manufacturer says a shaft is tip-stiff doesn't mean it is. Stiff compared to what? All the other shafts they make? All the shafts available in the market? The expertise of your fitter is invaluable in clearing the air when it comes to the shaft.

3. Shaft Flex

The flex of a shaft is measured in CPM (cycles per minute). It's a rating of the actual stiffness of the shaft and, amazingly, the industry has zero standards. One company's X-flex might be another's R-flex. How do you know? You don't! It's another reason why fitting and building is imperative to maximizing efficiency and performance.

4. Shaft Torque

Torque is a measurement of a shaft's ability to resist twisting around its own axis (torsional stiff-

ness). A good rule of thumb is that the stiffer and heavier the shaft, the lower the torque (the opposite is true for lighter, less-stiff shafts). Torque has lowered as clubhead sizes have increased in order to stop these 460cc-sized clubheads from rotating too much and give you a better chance of squaring the clubface. One of the great recent advances in golf equipment technology is the ability to lower torque while keeping overall shaft weight down.

5. Hoop Strength

This is a fairly new term and one of the biggest advances in graphite technology in a long time. Shaft companies have begun to realize that the faster you swing the more the shaft loses its roundness, wasting potential energy you're meant to transfer to the ball. Manufacturers have begun layering the graphite differently during the construction process—as well as using lighter and stronger materials—in order to help the shaft maintain its roundness longer and increase the amount of energy transferred to the ball.

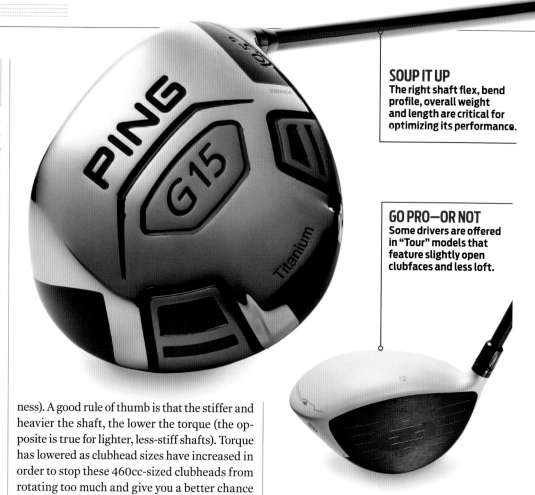

SOUP IT UP
The right shaft flex, bend profile, overall weight and length are critical for optimizing its performance.

GO PRO—OR NOT
Some drivers are offered in "Tour" models that feature slightly open clubfaces and less loft.

5 THINGS TO TAKE FROM THIS CHAPTER

1 Have an open mind when determining your fitting preference and your goals.

2 Use a launch monitor to determine technique and be fitted properly. Quantify your data.

3 There's a vast array of clubheads on the market. Test as many as you can.

4 Just switching to a new shaft can make your old driver behave like something that's brand new.

5 Know who will be building your club. Experience and knowledge count.

THE BUILD

Even if you nail the head and shaft combination that produces the maximum efficiency, how do you know it's going to be built correctly? The manner in which your club is put together is the absolute most important aspect of a driver fitting. If it's assembled incorrectly then all the testing you've done to this point will be worthless. A well-versed fitter knows what combinations can be obtained during the fitting and should only recommend combinations that can physically be made to exact specifications.

What to Watch for During Your Build

1. The **head weight** of the driver must be correct in order to achieve the proper swing weight at the desired length.

2. Grip weight must be correct to achieve the proper swing weight at the desired length and with the correct head weight.

3. The shaft must have the proper **starting flex** and be tipped if necessary.

4. The head can be re-weighted if necessary and, if so, the extra weight must be positioned in the correct spot or the **CG** will be compromised.

5. Make sure that the **"true loft"** of the driver is correct (just because it says 9.5 degrees doesn't mean that it is).

It's nearly impossible to perform a proper driver fitting without looking at all these parameters and options (the majority of which may be confusing to you), but finding the perfect combination of head, shaft, and grip comes down to this: Get fit by a brand-agnostic, reputable fitter/builder that offers a full array of demos and uses an accurate launch monitor. Make it someone you trust and who stands behinds his or her products. The promise of more yards and increased accuracy by finding the right combination of shaft and head specs, and building the club in an appropriate manner, is very real. ●

TRACKMAN™ LAUNCH OPTIMIZATION CHARTS

For every clubhead speed/attack angle combination there's an optimal launch condition that will give you the max possible yards. The only way to create these optimal launch conditions with your swing is to be fitted with a driver that produces the correct numbers.

MAXIMIZE CARRY

Club Speed (MPH)	Attack Angle (°)	Ball Speed (MPH)	Launch Angle (°)	Spin Rate (RPM)	Carry (YDS)	Total (YDS)
75	-5	104	14.6	3,722	143	166
75	0	107	16.3	3,121	154	178
75	5	108	19.2	2,720	164	187
80	-5	113	12.9	3,652	160	176
80	0	115	15.5	3,179	171	187
80	5	116	18.0	2,648	181	197
85	-5	121	11.9	3,669	175	199
85	0	123	14.5	3,164	187	211
85	5	124	17.0	2,596	197	223
90	-5	129	11.1	3,689	191	215
90	0	131	13.4	3,093	203	228
90	5	132	16.4	2,633	214	239
95	-5	137	9.9	3,626	207	243
95	0	138	12.7	3,114	219	244
95	5	140	15.7	2,595	231	256
100	-5	144	9.6	3,722	222	244
100	0	146	12.1	3,118	235	272
100	5	148	14.9	2,538	247	272
105	-5	152	8.7	3,675	237	260
105	0	154	11.2	3,038	251	275
105	5	155	14.5	2,563	263	288
110	-5	160	7.7	3,570	252	275
110	0	162	10.5	2,970	266	291
110	5	163	13.7	2,435	279	305
115	-5	168	7.0	3,548	266	290
115	0	170	9.8	2,919	281	306
115	5	171	13.0	2,358	295	321
120	-5	176	6.1	3,433	281	305
120	0	178	9.3	2,890	296	321
120	5	179	12.6	2,343	310	350

MAXIMIZE TOTAL DISTANCE

Club Speed (MPH)	Attack Angle (°)	Ball Speed (MPH)	Launch Angle (°)	Spin Rate (RPM)	Carry (YDS)	Total (YDS)
75	-5	107	11.8	3,214	140	182
75	0	109	13.0	2,506	147	195
75	5	111	15.3	1,976	156	206
80	-5	115	10.1	3,078	154	188
80	0	117	12.1	2,494	163	199
80	5	118	14.8	2,005	174	209
85	-5	123	9.3	3,110	169	215
85	0	125	11.7	2,568	180	228
85	5	126	14.0	1,964	189	241
90	-5	131	8.5	3,122	185	231
90	0	132	10.8	2,517	196	245
90	5	134	13.8	2,021	207	259
95	-5	138	7.9	3,144	201	247
95	0	140	10.5	2,565	213	262
95	5	141	13.0	1,948	223	276
100	-5	146	7.2	3,118	216	262
100	0	148	10.0	2,570	230	278
100	5	149	12.4	1,887	239	293
105	-5	154	6.4	3,071	231	278
105	0	156	9.1	2,461	243	294
105	5	157	11.7	1,810	254	309
110	-5	162	5.6	3,005	245	293
110	0	163	8.7	2,471	260	310
110	5	165	11.1	1,716	268	326
115	-5	170	5.3	3,030	261	307
115	0	171	8.0	2,396	274	325
115	5	172	10.7	1,681	285	342
120	-5	178	4.5	2,929	273	322
120	0	179	7.7	2,382	290	340
120	5	180	10.3	1,636	300	358

MEET THE EXPERTS

The ultimate team of driving experts represents the most trusted instructors, researchers and clubfitters in the game

MIKE ADAMS
Hamilton Farm G.C.
TOP 100 SINCE: 1996

Adams is a former PGA touring professional and known throughout the golf world as "Swing Doctor." He has authored some of the most important instruction books of the modern age (see *LAWs*), and is listed as a top instructor by both *GOLF Magazine* and *Golf Digest*. He also has won numerous teaching awards, including South Florida Teacher of the Year in 2001.
mikeadamsgolf.com

MIKE BENDER
Mike Bender Academy at Timacuan G.C.
TOP 100 SINCE: 1996

Mike Bender is a well-decorated instructor, having been named the 2009 PGA Teacher of the Year. He teaches players of all skill levels (most notably 2007 Masters champion Zach Johnson). An accomplished player in his own right, Bender was a three-time NCAA All American, and two-time NCAA Division III champion. He also spent three seasons on the PGA Tour (1987-1989).
mikebender.com

CHRIS DEMPSEY
Fuzion Golf

Chris Dempsey spent seven years building equipment for the top golfers on the PGA Tour. Equipment fit and built by Dempsey has proven itself with six major championships and over 20 regular season events on the PGA, LPGA and Champions tours. His dedication to the game and the equipment that fuels it led him to co-create the experience behind Fuzion Golf.
fuziongolf.com

ROGER FREDERICKS
Fredericks Golf

Roger Fredericks has taught over 20,000 golfers, including Arnold Palmer, Gary Player and Jack Nicklaus. A leader in the golf fitness movement, he founded the Del Mar Golf College in San Diego, and has studied the game with such notable instructors as Paul Runyan, Eddie Merrins and Phil Rodgers. Fredericks currently operates out of La Costa Resort & Spa in Carlsbad, Calif.
fredericksgolf.com

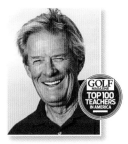

JIM HARDY
Plane Truth Golf
TOP 100 TEACHER: 1996

One of the game's most respected teachers, Hardy has done many things in golf, including winning All-American honors at OSU in the '60s, playing on the PGA Tour in the '70s, and winning the National Teacher of the Year award in 2007. Hardy has taught dozens of PGA Tour pros and mentored top-level instructors, and is well-known for his best-selling book, *Plane Truth for Golfers*.
planetruthgolf.com

JAMES LEITZ
Pinewood C.C.

Leitz has been the head pro at Pinewood C.C. for 30 years. He has won a number of PGA accolades, including the 2006 Barbato/Thomas Lifetime Achievement Award presented by the Louisiana section, and the 2002 and 2005 Gulf States Teacher of the Year Award. He's one of only eight PGA Certified Clubfitting pros who's also an authorized instructor of the *Golfing Machine*.
leitzgolf.com

JIM McLEAN
Jim McLean Golf School/Doral Golf Resort
TOP 100 SINCE: 1996

The 1994 PGA Teacher of the Year, Jim McLean is best known for his ground-breaking use of video and his X-Factor theories. Playing achievements include being one of very few people to qualify for the U.S. Junior, U.S. Amateur, U.S. Open and U.S. Senior Open (he also made the cut at the Masters). His training grounds at Doral are the stuff of legend in instruction circles.
jimmclean.com

ROBERT NEAL, PH.D.
Golf BioDynamics

Robert Neal's Golf BioDynamics team (founded in Australia) has worked with numerous Tour professionals, the Australian Institute of Sport and various international sporting associations. An expert in biomechanics, Neal was a highly ranked amateur player for over 20 years, placing him in the perfect position to provide analysis on the inner workings of the swing.
golfbiodynamics.com

DAVE PHILLIPS
Titleist Performance Institute
TOP 100 SINCE: 2001

Dave Phillips not only works for the most advanced golf fitness operation in the world (TPI), he helped found it. His background in computerized swing analysis and biomechanics allows him to instruct in a very understandable way, and create a clear picture of what happens in the swing. He has worked with PGA Tour players Hal Sutton and Peter Jacobsen, among many others.
mytpi.com

JIM SUTTIE, PH.D.
TwinEagles Club/Cog Hill G.C.
TOP 100 SINCE: 1996

For more than 30 years, Jim "Doc" Suttie has been improving the games of golfers just like you—and more than a handful of Tour players along the way. His biomechanical research has culminated in some of golf's most revolutionary teaching methods. He's one of the world's most-respected golf instructors. In 2000, he was named the PGA Teacher of the Year.
jimsuttie.com

JON TATTERSALL
Terminus Club
TOP 100 SINCE: 2007

PGA member and former British PGA member Jon Tattersall began his U.S. teaching career in 1988. He opened the The Gary Smith Learning Center in Atlanta before launching Golf Performance Partners with performance specialist Todd Townes in 2006. He has coached winners on all major tours, and is a member of Nike Golf's Bill Bowerman Advisory Staff.
terminusclub.com

T.J. TOMASI, PH.D.
PGA Center for Learning & Performance
TOP 100 SINCE: 1999

An author of over a dozen books, numerous blogs and a syndicated column, T.J. Tomasi is one of the most widely published authorities on the swing. He holds a Ph.D. and Masters in Education, and it's estimated that he has taught 50,000+ lessons. In addition to his current instruction duties, Tomasi serves as Program Director for *GOLF Magazine's* Top 100 Teachers in America.
tjtomasi.com

E.A. TISCHLER
New Horizons Golf Approach

Former college golf captain and playing pro E.A. Tischler has taught full-time since 1991, with lesson tees in Hawaii and his native northern California. He has authored 18 instruction books and developed his own theories on improvement, highlighted by the "P3 Golf Biomechanics System." A former +4.5 handicap, Tischler can also practice what he preaches.
newhorizonsgolf.com

KEVIN WALKER
Fuzion Golf
TOP 100: 1996-2008

Capping a brilliant full-time teaching career at some of the country's finest courses that landed him on every conceivable "Top Teacher" list, Kevin Walker helped launch Fuzion Golf to better marry the benefits of instruction and fitting. A former Horton Smith Award winner, Walker has taught several high-profile players including Brad Faxon and Tom Kite.
fuziongolf.com

CHRIS WELCH
ZenoLink

Biomedical engineer Chris Welch is one of the most sought-after performance consultants in golf. In 1995, he launched Human Performance Technologies (HPT), the first company to provide affordable and applicable 3D motion analysis. He's currently founder and CEO of ZenoLink (Ithaca, N.Y.), a spin-off of HTP that provides 3D analysis services across all sports.
zenolink.com

BRIAN YEE, P.T.
Terminus Club

Sporting two masters, Terminus Club's Director of Physical Therapy Brian Yee also instructs part-time at Georgia State University, devoting much of his research to recurring back and neck pain and biomechanical extremity injuries. He's the founder of Motion Stability, LLC, an organization that trains professionals and patients to reduce these maladies.
terminusclub.com

CREDITS

EDITOR
David M. Clarke

CREATIVE DIRECTOR
Paul Crawford

EXECUTIVE EDITOR
Eamon Lynch

ART DIRECTOR
Paul Ewen

MANAGING EDITORS
David DeNunzio (Instruction)
Gary Perkinson (Production)
Robert Sauerhaft (Equipment)

EDITOR AT LARGE
Connell Barrett

DEPUTY MANAGING EDITOR
Michael Chwasky (Instruction & Equipment)

SENIOR EDITORS
Alan Bastable, Michael Walker Jr.
Joseph Passov (Travel/Course Rankings)

SENIOR EDITOR, GOLF MAGAZINE CUSTOM PUBLISHING
Thomas Mackin

DEPUTY ART DIRECTOR
Karen Ha

PHOTO EDITORS
Carrie Boretz (Associate)
Jesse Reiter (Assistant)

SENIOR WRITERS
Michael Bamberger, Damon Hack, Cameron Morfit,
Alan Shipnuck, Gary Van Sickle

ASSOCIATE EDITOR
Steven Beslow

ASSISTANT EDITOR
Jessica Marksbury

PUBLISHER
Dick Raskopf

DIRECTOR OF BUSINESS DEVELOPMENT
Brad J. Felenstein

SPECIAL THANKS
Christine Austin, Jeremy Biloon, Glenn Buonocore, Malati
Chavali, Jim Childs, Rose Cirrincione, Caroline DeNunzio,
Davey DeNunzio, Dominick DeNunzio, Harvey Ewen,
Jacqueline Fitzgerald, Christine Font, Mark Hackett, Lauren
Hall, Carrie Hertan, Malena Jones, Suzanne Janso, Brynn
Joyce, Mona Li, Robert Marasco, Kimberly Marshall, Amy
Migliaccio, Nina Mistry, Kimberely Posa, Dave Rozzelle, Ilene
Schrieder, Adrianna Tierno, Sydney Webber, Vanessa Wu,
Hamilton Farm G.C., Old Palm G.C.

EDITOR, TIME INC. SPORTS GROUP
Terry McDonell

MANAGING EDITOR, SI.COM
Paul Fichtenbaum

MANAGING EDITOR, SI GOLF GROUP
James P. Herre

PRESIDENT, TIME INC. SPORTS GROUP
Mark Ford

V.P., PUBLISHER
Frank Wall

SENIOR V.P., CONSUMER MARKETING
Nate Simmons

V.P., COMMUNICATIONS AND DEVELOPMENT
Scott Novak

ASSOC. PUBLISHER, MKTG. AND CREATIVE SERVICES
Charlie Saunders

SENIOR V.P., FINANCE
Elissa Fishman

V.P., FINANCE
Peter Greer

CONSUMER MARKETING DIRECTOR
Ann Marie Doherty

V.P., OPERATIONS
Brooke Twyford

LEGAL
Judith Margolin

HUMAN RESOURCES DIRECTOR
Liz Matilla

GOLF.com

EXECUTIVE EDITOR
Charlie Hanger

EXECUTIVE PRODUCER
Christopher Shade

DEPUTY EDITOR
David Dusek

SENIOR PRODUCERS
Ryan Reiterman, Jeff Ritter

ASSOCIATE PRODUCER
Kevin Cunningham

PUBLISHER
Richard Fraiman

GENERAL MANAGER
Steven Sandonato

EXECUTIVE DIRECTOR, MARKETING SERVICES
Carol Pittard

EXECUTIVE DIRECTOR, RETAIL & SPECIAL SALES
Tom Mifsud

EXECUTIVE DIRECTOR, NEW PRODUCT DEVELOPMENT
Peter Harper

DIRECTOR, BOOKAZINE DEVELOPMENT & MARKETING
Laura Adam

PUBLISHING DIRECTOR
Joy Butts

ASSISTANT GENERAL COUNSEL
Helen Wan

BOOK PRODUCTION MANAGER
Susan Chodakiewicz

DESIGN & PREPRESS MANAGER
Anne-Michelle Gallero

BRAND MANAGER
Allison Parker

ASSOCIATE PREPRESS MANAGER
Alex Voznesenskiy

THE BEST DRIVING INSTRUCTION BOOK EVER!
by the *GOLF Magazine* Driving Instructors

EDITOR
David DeNunzio

ART DIRECTION/DESIGN
Paul Ewen

PHOTOGRAPHY
Angus Murray *(Instruction)*, Schecter Lee *(Gear)*
Robert Beck *(pp. 54 inset, 162 inset)*,
John Biever *(p. 102 inset)*, Fred Vuich *(pp. 6 TM, TR,
BR; 30-31; 39 T; 40 M, B; 41 T; 54-55)*

ILLUSTRATION
Phil Franké *(pp. 83-87)*

IMAGING
Geoffrey A. Michaud (Director, SI Imaging)
Dan Larkin, Robert M. Thompson,
Gerald Burke, Neil Clayton

EDITORIAL CONSULTANTS
Mike Adams, Michael Chwasky

VIDEO PRODUCTION
John Ledesma/Optimism Media Group